Home Repair and Maintenance

Home Repair and Maintenance

Tony Wilkins

Newnes Technical Books

Newnes Technical Books
is an imprint of the Butterworth Group
which has principal offices in
London, Sydney, Toronto, Wellington, Durban and Boston

First published 1977
Reprinted 1981

ISBN 0 408 00242 5

Typeset by Butterworths Litho Preparation Department
Printed and Bound in England by
Hazell Watson & Viney Ltd, Aylesbury, Bucks

Preface

A home will not look after itself, and the occupant must be prepared to do battle with damp, rust and corrosion, fading, peeling, wormholes, leaks, blown fuses—and much more besides.

Professional services are expensive and from this stems the great incentive to tackle the work yourself; if you can reduce costs to materials only, this will have two immediate effects. First, you will have money to do more and, second, you may have money available with which to buy better quality materials and add the frills.

The term do-it-yourself encompasses a very wide field of activity, and there is much to learn. It is not always easy, but once new skills have been mastered d-i-y becomes rewarding and satisfying.

All the books in the d-i-y series have been written by people with very considerable practical experience, and all have been involved in feature-writing for DIY magazine over the years. The authors have also been responsible for dealing with hundreds of readers' queries—which has given them an invaluable insight into the problems encountered in and about the house.

I'm sure you will find their advice invaluable. May I wish you success in all you undertake.

Tony Wilkins
Editor, 'Do-it-Yourself' Magazine

Contents

Introduction

For most people, the purchase of a home of one's own is the biggest financial investment we will make in a lifetime, and we are likely to spend most of our working life paying for it. Even so, there are few who regret the decision to get a place of their very own. A place you can call home; where you can shut the door on the world.

Unfortunately, beneath the sentiment lies the hard reality. All property, from the most humble up to the palatial, depreciates with the passing of time. Wood tries to rot away; metal rusts; masonry flakes and cracks; colours fade. When taking on the responsibility of a home of your own, accept the fact that unless you spend time and money on maintenance, your asset will quickly depreciate in value. The more the neglect, the faster the process of breakdown will move.

Regular periods of maintenance and redecoration are of far more value than infrequent purges. The costs are less; the work is easier, and the chances of the weather really getting into the actual fabric of the house are reduced.

Maintenance is also part of the investment programme, because when you come to sell your property you can be sure it will hold its value, and that it will stand up to the private survey.

The purpose of this book is twofold. First to point out the many areas where repair work and maintenance may be necessary, and second to introduce to you the tools and materials you will need to carry out the work.

In the latter respect we are very privileged. There is now a whole d-i-y industry geared to meeting our needs in both excellent tools and materials. Processes have been very much simplified, and products are designed to be effective and easy to use. In many cases throughout the text you will find that detailed instructions on the use of particular tools and materials are not given in full. This is because clear instructions are given with the products when purchased, and it is a waste of space to repeat them here. It is vital that instructions given are studied carefully and carried out faithfully, for it is in this area that so much d-i-y work founders. Poor preparation, careless application, the use of the wrong tools, all add up to an inferior job.

When you come to the larger jobs once looked upon as the preserve of the tradesman, the hire shop comes into its own. These shops will offer you the same facilities that they offer to the professional, giving clear instructions on equipment you would not want to buy, but which can take the strain out of the work and speed it up very considerably.

This book does not cover decorating, as this subject is dealt with in detail in the companion volume ***Home Decorating.*** Similarly, plumbing and electrics are dealt with in considerable detail in two separate books in this new series.

To summarise, it is essential to have a system. Start a reference book of all the repairs done to your home and the date when tackled. This will be invaluable as time passes—both to highlight which areas still need to be dealt with, and as a reminder of when to return to vulnerable areas in the future.

FOR YOUR REFERENCE

Below is listed a good basic tool kit which will see you through most repair jobs about the house. But you will find many others which can be added as you progress in certain fields. All those mentioned here are referred to in the following chapter.

Work bench, fixed or portable
Steel rule
Steel tape
Try square
Tenon saw
Hacksaw and blades
General purpose saw
Cross cut saw
Plane with disposable blades
Shaping tools
Wheel brace and set of twist drills
Screwdrivers, for single slot, Phillips and Pozidriv* screws
Bench vice—can be clamp-on
Wrench
Pincers
Pliers, large and fine nose
Claw hammer
Pin hammer
Chisels
Craft knife
Masonry drills
Adjustable spanner
Soldering iron
Wire brush
Safety glasses
Files
Spirit level
Marking knife
Marking gauge
Chain wrench
Tinsnips
Putty knife
Nail punch
Bevel
Smooth plane
Brace and set of bits

Spiral ratchet screwdriver
G cramps
Club hammer
Glass cutter
Tile cutter
Trowels, large and small
Soft face hammer
Tape—surveyor's
Grindstone
Blowtorch
Welder
Nut splitter
Riveting kit
Case opener
Power drill
– plus the following attachments:
  Sander
  Saw—circular
  Saw—jig
  Vertical drill stand
  Spray gun
  Rasps
  Flexible drive
  Speed reducer
  Right-angle drive

Integral power tools include:
  Jigsaw
  Circular saw
  Band saw
  Router
  Belt sander
  Grinder
  Floor sander
  Orbital sander
  Planer

*The name Supadrive is replacing Posidriv, but the latter is used throughout this book.

Chapter 1
The tools you will need

A good selection of tools is essential for repair and maintenance work. If you are just setting up a kit, aim to get into good habits and use your tools for the job they were designed. A good chisel is not a screwdriver or a tyre lever. A coal hammer is not designed to drive nails, and pliers won't undo nuts very well. I have seen all these tools used in the ways described!

Buy the very best tools you can afford—even if it means buying less. A good tool will last more than a lifetime if looked after properly, and it will do a job well. Cheap, bargain-price tools may range from inefficient to dangerous, and in the long run they save no money as they will need replacing.

Store your tools so that they are easy to find. Ensure that they do not bang against each other and become dull or blunt, and keep them dry so that they do not rust. Keep edge tools sharp at all times, for apart from cutting badly, a blunt tool is dangerous in that it is much more prone to slipping.

If you are unable to sharpen your own saws and drills, take them to a good tool shop and have the job done properly. It makes an incredible difference to the efficiency. Remember that some tools, like chisels and plane irons, still come needing a final sharpening. For this you will need a stone, and a simple sharpening jig which holds a blade at the correct angle while it is rubbed on the stone.

Tool safety

When using tools, it is absolutely vital to cultivate the right attitude, for if used thoughtlessly or carelessly they can be dangerous. Make sure all tools are kept out of the reach of small children. Do not allow children in your working area unless under supervision.

Any tools connected to the electricity supply should be disconnected if left, even if for a few moments. Small children are inquisitive, and this could lead to dreadful accidents. Keep soldering irons out of reach while cooling; they are extremely hot even when they appear cold.

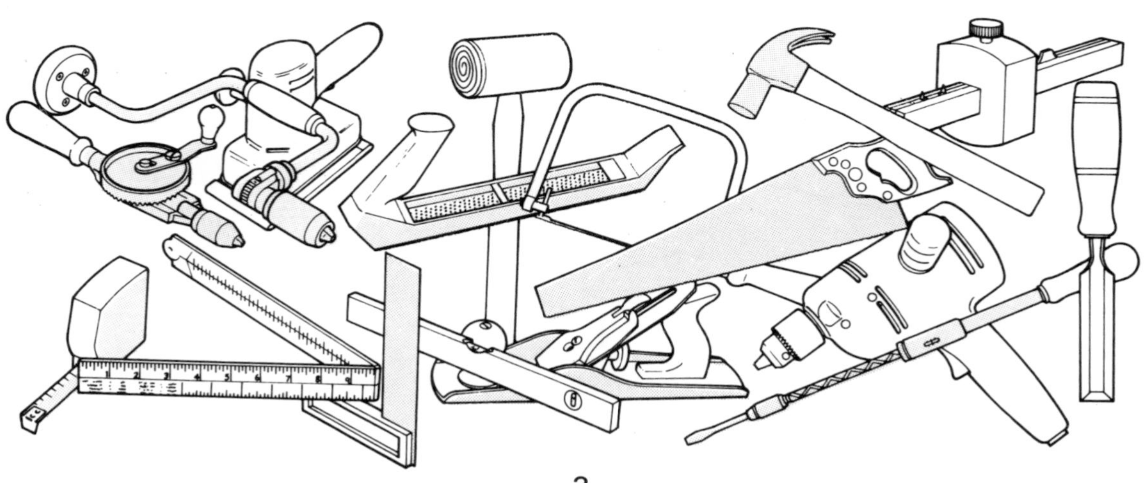

Some of the tools you will need. Buy the best you can afford

Where a tool is held in one hand—for example a knife or chisel—always cut ***away*** from your other hand. This means siting it behind the direction of cut. Never ignore or remove guards, and when using a tool like a power saw, use scrap wood to push short pieces past the blade. Take extreme care with abrasive cutting discs, these are as lethal as any saw blade, yet there is no form of guard supplied when used in a power tool.

Always wear protective glasses when doing such jobs as wire-brushing metal or masonry or when using a grinding wheel. Similarly protect your eyes when using chemicals such as paint stripper or rust remover. Special safety goggles are sold by good tool shops which are light and easy to wear, yet which give excellent protection.

Never use chisels or files without a correct handle. The tang will drive into your hand very easily.

Always have adequate ventilation when using adhesives with heavy vapours, and never use petrol for cleaning. Take great care with blowtorches and never leave inflammable materials lying around.

One moment's thoughtfulness can save a lifetime of remorse.

Left, a rigid workbench for general repair work. Right, a useful folding workbench

Workbench

If you have room in a workshop or a large garage, a good solid workbench with a woodworker's vice and a small metalworker's vice will prove invaluable as a base for repair jobs. It should have a clear uncluttered top and stout legs which hold it firm when you are sawing or planing.

The great problem with a fixed bench is that it is often difficult to handle or turn long strips of material because of the proximity of the walls. It will help if there is room to pull the bench away from the wall.

Light is also important, and if daylight is not available, adequate artificial light is necessary. As well as fixed lights, adjustable lights are an asset so that you can lose awkward shadows.

In recent years the attitude towards the workbench has been transformed by the introduction of a portable bench. Adjustable to one of two heights, this has two large wood jaws which act as both powerful vice and working surface. Grooves in the jaws make it possible to hold bars or tubes, and special plastic stops can be positioned to hold sheet materials.

The beauty of this new approach is that the bench folds flat—small enough to be housed in the boot of a car, or hung out of the way on a garage wall. This means it

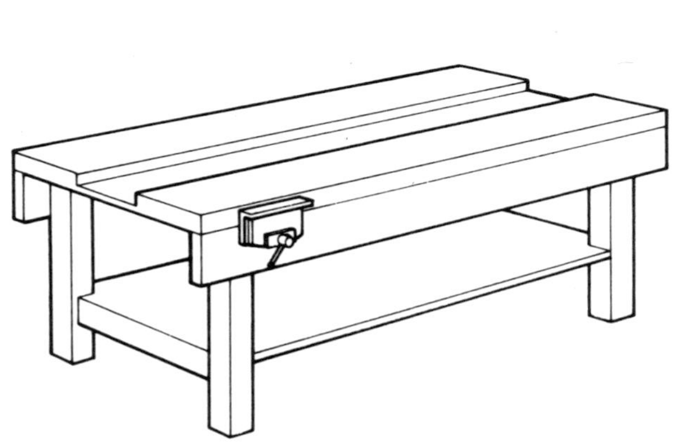

can be taken to the job in very many instances, whether indoors or out, to tackle anything from pipe threading to holding a door while it is trimmed to size.

As well as normal uses, various power tool equipment can be firmly held by making up suitable blocks of wood to be gripped in the jaws. For example, a vertical drill stand can be mounted on the bench top in this way, giving a very secure mounting.

Basic tools

Steel rule

This will be useful for accurate measurements over short distances, and it will offer a true edge for marking with a knife or cutting. Keep this blade slightly oiled to avoid rusting. A wood ruler is no substitute for this tool.

Steel tape

Choose a tape at least 3 m long, and preferably with both imperial and metric markings. One with a lock is useful so that the blade can be held extended with no hand on the other end. A dressmaking cloth tape is no substitute for a steel tape.

Try square

A try square will enable you to mark accurate right angles, provided it has a true surface to be positioned against. It is also useful for checking items like picture frames, table legs and shelf brackets before finally fixing in place. A try square with sliding metal rule is useful as this combines the services of square, depth gauge and 45° angle marking.

Tenon saw

This has fine teeth set in a blade strengthened by a special metal strip running along its back. Choose one about 25 cm long. It is ideal for cutting small wood sections and for joint cutting. It is not suited to cutting sheet materials as the stiffened back gets in the way.

Hacksaw

Frame sizes vary and it would pay you to invest in two. A small frame with blades to match for fine metal cutting work, and a larger frame and blades for heavier work and sheet cutting. Apart from the usual frames, simple grip handles are available which will hold a piece of hacksaw blade. Such a tool is very useful in confined areas where a normal frame would get in the way. Note that a blade mounted in this way is always fixed so the cut is made on the *pull* stroke and not the push. A push cut would bend the blade. When fixing blades in a hacksaw frame always obey the instructions with regard to blade tensioning.

Apart from standard blades, graduated blades, ranging from coarse to fine, are available. This simplifies starting a cut prior to rapid cutting of material.

Multi-purpose saw

This is a very useful new saw for d-i-y use, as it has a blade designed for cutting wood or metal. Most saws can be adjusted to any one of a number of blade angles in relation to the handle.

The saw is ideal for reducing second-hand timber which may well contain old nails. It is also useful for cutting sheet materials where the accuracy of a hand saw is not required.

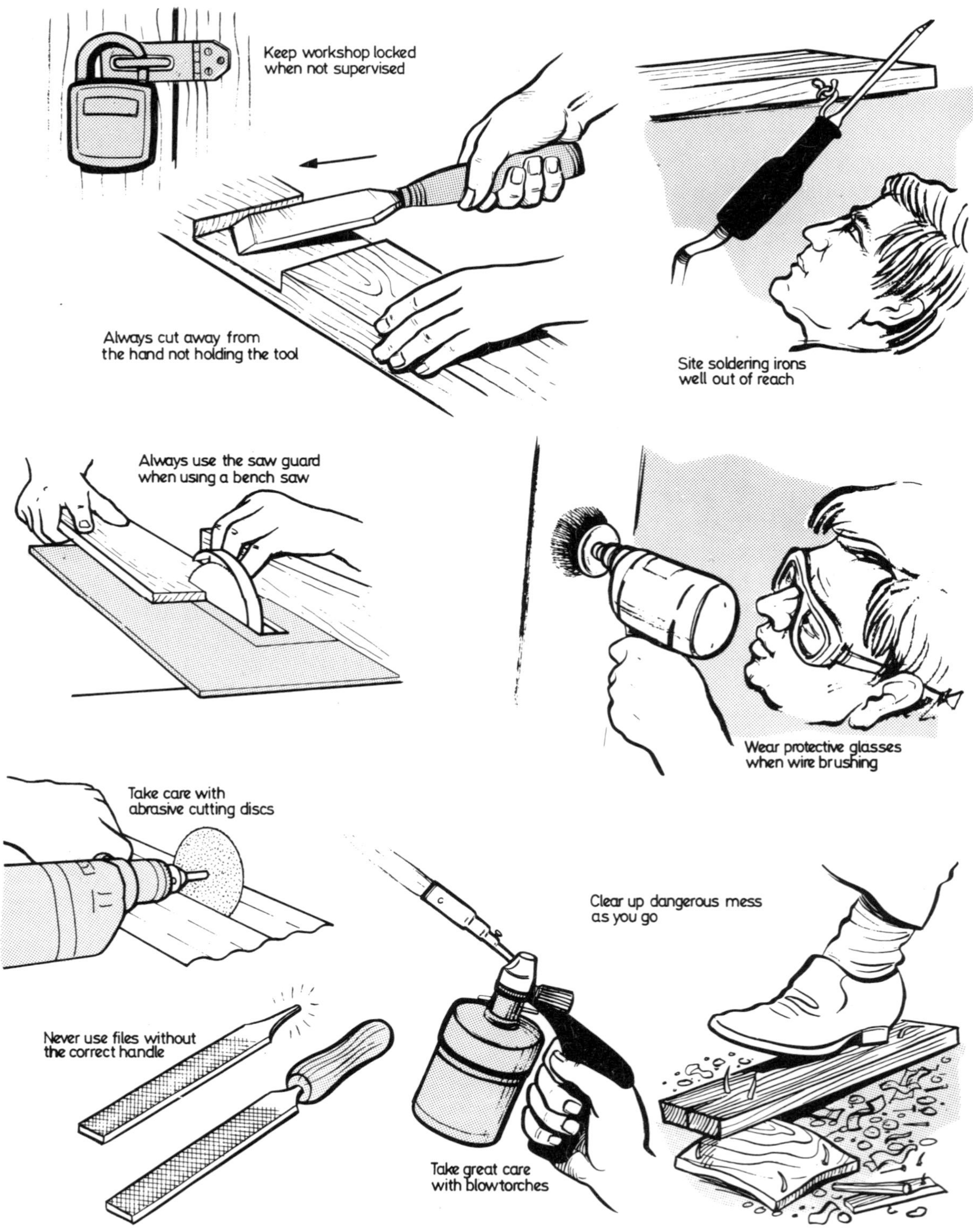

Care and safety is important. Here are a few tips to keep you accident-free

Cross-cut saw

This saw, about 60 cm long, is designed for general wood cutting mainly across the grain of the wood. Its teeth are designed to cut through the wood fibres; it does not work very efficiently along the wood grain. If you plan to do along-grain cutting quite often, a rip saw should be added to your kit. It should not be used on timber containing nails as the teeth will be very easily blunted or damaged.

Disposable blade plane

Another tool designed for the d-i-y enthusiast, this plane has blades rather resembling tough razor blades. It is easily adjusted, needs no sharpening, and as soon as a blade is blunted, it may be removed and a new one inserted.

For many d-i-y projects, prepared timber is accurate enough to make frames, without planing. But the plane comes into its own for fine cutting to size and making things fit accurately.

Shaping tools

Closely allied to the plane is the shaping tool which, without the finesse of a plane will remove timber quickly and accurately. It may also act as a rasp, shaping wood to any contour. If you examine the blade closely you will see the perforated blade has dozens of fine chisel-like blades which cut in turn into the wood. A special blade is produced for metal cutting.

Various sizes and shapes are available, and two or three will prove invaluable.

One type, with a rasp-like blade has a handle which swivels to form either a plane or file. The blade can also be tensioned to form a curve.

Wheel brace

When fixing timber, it is wise to pre-drill it so that no pressure is exerted by screws causing it to split. This rule also applies in hardwoods when nailing. For this drilling you need a wheel brace and a set of twist drills, which may also be used for drilling metal. Add a rose countersink bit so that the heads of countersunk screws can be taken flush with the surface of the wood.

Be gentle when drilling with very fine twist drills. They snap easily if the drill is moved out of vertical while drilling.

Screwdrivers

A collection of screwdrivers will be needed for various repair work, and the general rule is that the screwdriver tip should fit neatly into the slot and wherever possible fit the width of the slot. If the tip is too wide, it could damage the surrounding area and if too narrow, the tip will be strained and twisted. The tip should be square, with sharply defined edges.

For electrical work you will find drivers with insulated handles tested up to high voltages—but at no time should you use this as an excuse to touch live equipment. It is purely a safety measure. You will encounter three main slot designs today:

Single slot. The standard screw slot requiring a standard screwdriver.

Phillips cross slot. The screwdriver tip has a cruciform shape which fits into the slot, giving a far more positive location with no danger of slipping. These have been in use for many years.

Pozidriv screws. This has a more sophisticated cruciform slot with sloping sides and is gradually replacing the Phillips slot. If used with the best Pozidriv drivers, there is the considerable advantage that a

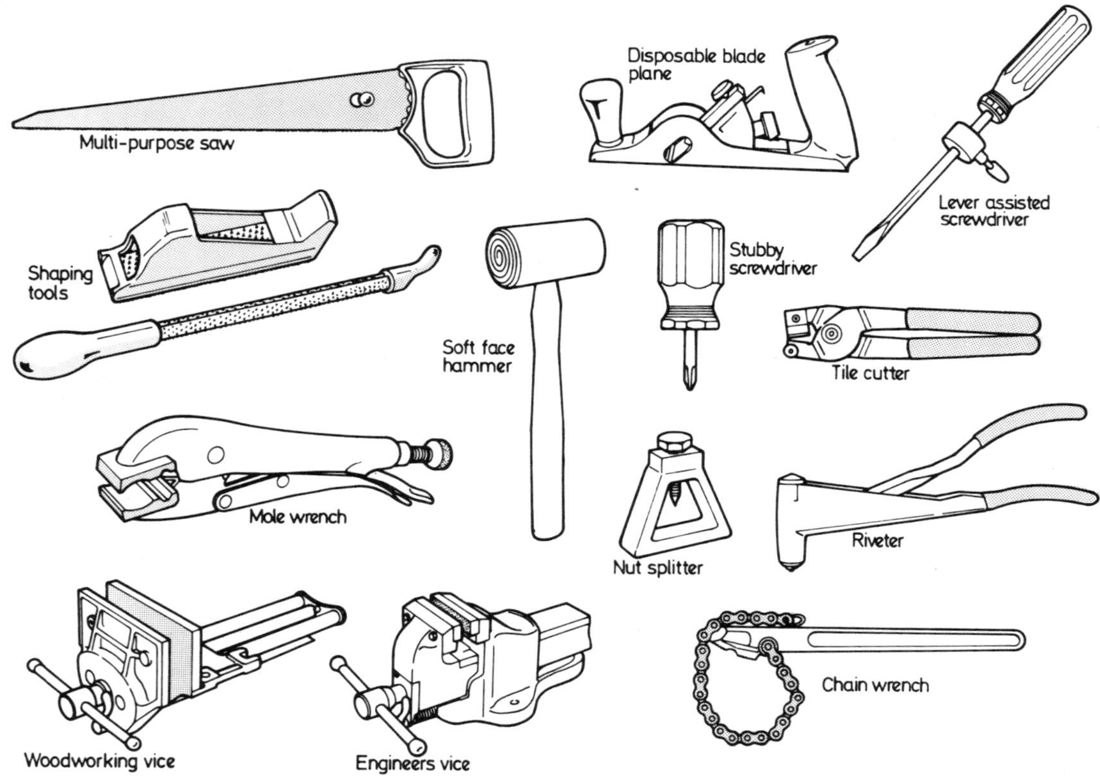

Here are some of the tools you may not have encountered so far. Worthy additions to a kit

screw can be held locked on the end of the driver. This makes it possible to insert screws in awkward places, and apply pressure without holding the screw in your hand until it is started. Cheap Pozidriv drivers should be avoided as they lose this advantage through their poor fit.

You will need three drivers to cover the range of screw sizes in the Pozidriv range, and you will find a really fine tip invaluable when you encounter items like fine piano hinges and certain modern domestic appliances held by the smallest Pozidriv screws.

Back to drivers generally, a long blade helps with good driving, but there will be occasions when there is no room to manoeuvre a long blade. Add a stubby screwdriver or two to your kit to meet these circumstances—and a couple of right-angle driver blades for the really difficult locations.

If you need extra leverage to undo screws, drivers are available which have a lever which can be slipped over the screwdriver blade. Undue force should never be used to do up screws. You can turn a head off a screw in this way.

Vice

Apart from a vice fixed to a workbench, it helps to have a clamp-on vice which can be fixed to any firm surface, such as a kitchen table. This will be useful for smaller indoor repair jobs. It is worth investing in a vice with interchangeable jaws, for when dealing with soft metals or plastics, rubber jaws are far kinder. Such a unit is not really designed for heavy jobs like sawing and planing, for the clamp cannot hold it firm enough.

Snap-on wrench

This type of wrench can be adjusted by means of a screw so that it will snap firmly on to any object, holding it in a vice-like grip. This has the advantage of leaving one hand free to hold the wrench without applying pressure while the other hand uses file or spanner. You can also buy a simple clamp into which the wrench drops, converting it into a miniature vice, ideal for holding small items while they are worked on.

It is not wise to use such a wrench as a spanner, as the hardened jaws can easily damage the flats of nuts.

Pincers

Pincers are very useful for pulling nails and tacks. Where you encounter large nails, use the claw of a claw hammer instead.

Pliers

You will need a heavy duty pair of pliers for gripping and pulling. The pliers will also have two keen cutting edges for cutting wire, plus two aligning slots which cut wire with a shearing action.

You should add a pair of fine-nose pliers for dealing with more delicate work. Never over-strain the nose section or they lose their effective grip.

Claw hammer

This combines a good striking face with a well-shaped claw with a vee slot. The slot should be sharp enough to grip a nail firmly while it is pulled. There is a choice of wood handle or hollow metal handle with rubber grip. The latter is the more comfortable tool to use.

Pin hammer

Designed to drive small nails, pins and tacks, this is a much lighter tool to handle. It should be kept for the lighter jobs and not abused. The flat end is called a pein, and it is designed to tap into place small nails and pins held between the fingers.

There is also a simple device called a pin push. This consists of a handle to which is attached a hollow tube in which a small nail can be held by magnetic attraction. A smart push on the handle is all that is required to drive the pin home.

Chisels

These do not get so much use as they used to when most things in wood were held together by joints cut with saw and chisel. Even so it will pay to have a set of three or four. Choose the bevel edge type in 6 mm, 12 mm, 19 mm and 25 mm sizes. Also buy plastic caps to protect the tips.

As mentioned earlier, chisels do not come sharpened, and you will need a stone and a honing gauge to get them in working order and to keep them really keen.

Buy a mallet with which to hit the chisel handle. Never use an ordinary hammer for this job.

Craft knife

Choose a type with interchangeable blades, and buy some spares. Take extreme care as such a knife is razor-sharp. Special blades for carpet and vinyl cutting, and for scoring laminates are available.

The carpet blade is curved and has a blunt tip so it cuts without touching the floor. A laminate blade scratches more than cuts, after which the laminate is snapped.

Masonry drills

When drilling into walls, you need to use special drills with a hardened tip. It is very easy to recognise the difference if you compare the tip with a standard twist drill. Buy good masonry drills, and get them sharpened as soon as they start to 'whistle' in a hole without cutting. You will find that the drills relate to wall plug and screw sizes, and you should always match drill, plug and screws when fixing.

Adjustable spanner

It is wise to buy two spanners. One for fine work and one for heavy work. Buy good spanners with no 'play' in the jaws and which need little effort to open and close.

If you plan to tackle plumbing work, you will need to invest in a much larger spanner or wrench, as most adjustable types do not open far enough to take the nuts on sanitary ware.

Soldering iron

A pencil-tip type of iron will cope with most domestic work, but it will not retain enough heat for dealing with large sheets of metal where there is considerable heat dissipation. Similarly, for really fine electronic work you will need a much smaller iron or you risk spoiling components and circuits.

Buy a roll of cored solder which has a flux inbuilt. The flux is necessary to ensure sound joints.

Wire brush

This is invaluable for removing scale from rust or brushing off surplus mortar, and it should always be used in conjunction with a pair of safety goggles or glasses. These protect the eyes against flying particles. Good goggles are shatterproof, even when struck quite hard.

Files

It will pay you to make a collection of files—from coarse to fine, flat, half-round, triangular and circular. These will prove invaluable for small adjustments to metal components. Never use files without a proper handle as the tangs can be very dangerous.

Files are for metalwork and have little effect on wood. The wood equivalent is the rasp, which has coarser teeth which are easier to clear. A couple of rasps are a good investment for fine shaping areas where a plane would be difficult to use. See also 'shaping tools' described earlier.

Spirit level

An invaluable tool for many jobs such as: checking that shelves are level; that wall tiles start horizontal; checking the fall on guttering and paths and that posts are set truly vertical. Choose a type with both horizontal and vertical checks and, for a little extra, you can have one with a bubble which can be set to any chosen angle. For checking over longer distances, you need a dead true batten on which to stand the level.

Marking knife

When working to fine tolerances, a pencil is not all that accurate. A marking knife is better–and it gives a start for things like the chisel and saw. Keep it for marking.

One or two woodworking pencils are an asset too. These have flat heads which can be sharpened to a fine spade-like point.

Additional tools

The tools mentioned so far will see you through most jobs, but there are others you will probably wish to add as your scope of work increases. Here are a few.

Marking gauge

If you plan to make joints, however simple, you will benefit from an adjustable marking gauge. The body can be adjusted, then a steel pin does the actual marking on the wood. There is a more elaborate model called the mortise gauge which has two pins, and as its name implies it is designed for marking out mortise and tenon joints.

Chain wrench

This is invaluable if you tackle any pipe-work, whether plumbing or central heating. It will grip or turn pipes of a wide range of diameters far more effectively than a wrench.

Tinsnips

Designed for cutting and trimming sheet metals, tinsnips are invaluable in many repair jobs where metal sheet or perforated materials are used.

Putty knife

The ideal tool for cutting and smoothing putty to the correct angle. There are variations on a theme now for amateur use to ensure the correct finishing angle, and one of these could be added if you do not have much success with a knife.

Nail punch

This is for setting nails below a surface without bruising the wood. It can be used wherever the nail heads are to be hidden by a wood stopping or filler.

Adjustable bevel

This tool is useful for fine woodworking where angles need to be accurately marked.

Smooth plane

Again, this is a tool for the woodworker who wants accurate surfaces. It is worth investing in a smooth plane 20 to 25 cm long. This is the shortest of the wood-working planes, and the enthusiast may wish to invest in a jack plane and a jointer plane. The general rule is that the longer the plane base, the more accurately it cuts flat surfaces.

Brace and bits

This is the tool that will be used for boring holes larger than can be tackled with twist drills. Its chuck is designed to take bits with square shanks, and bits come in a variety of sizes. Alternatively you can invest in one or two expansive bits, where the cutter can be adjusted to give holes of different sizes.

You can also buy screwdriver bits to fit the brace, and these are invaluable for turning large screws which have been over-tightened. Be warned when using such a driver to tighten screws that you can very easily turn the head off a screw with this tool.

Spiral ratchet screwdriver

The action used with this screwdriver is to pump the handle to and fro, which in turn causes the driver blade to rotate, either driving in or loosening the screw. It is ideal for repetition work with prepared holes. You have a choice of bits, including a small range of drills for fine hole making.

G cramps

Two or three of these will prove useful for holding components firmly to a base while being worked on. They offer a simple way of holding sheet materials while using a power drill to make holes or cut shapes. They will also kill vibration when using a power jig saw, and can be used to prevent a cut closing when sawing sheet material.

Club hammer

This hammer has a heavy, solid head designed to exert considerable force on steel chisels. Used with a steel chisel, it is the tool used for cutting paving slabs, splitting and channeling concrete or making holes in brickwork. Again, when using this tool, it is wise to wear safety glasses to avoid flying pieces damaging your eyes. For accurate cutting of paving slabs, there is a wide version of the steel chisel called a bolster, and it is a worthwhile investment for garden work.

Glass cutter

Buy a good wheel cutter. It is far easier for the amateur to use than the more expensive diamond cutter, and just as effective when used properly. You can buy one with interchangeable wheels if you plan to do a lot of glasscutting, but a single wheel model is adequate for most people. The notches on the cutter are for nibbling away narrow areas of glass.

Tile cutter

The easiest type to use rather resembles a very thin, pointed pencil, and the hardened tip will score the surface of a tile very easily. A more sophisticated type has a wheel cutter and a pliers action clamp which will hold and snap a tile along the cut. Yet another type offers a base with a wheel cutter projecting upwards over which the tile is run.

Trowels

Invest in both a small and a large trowel. The large trowel for handling mixed mortar and concrete, when tackling repairs, and the small trowel for finer repair work and for re-pointing brickwork and mortar. If you do repair work to rendering and plasterwork, you will need to add a hawk for carrying your mix, and a float for spreading it. The float is not an easy tool to use, and plastering requires very considerable expertise.

Soft-face hammer

Choose a hammer with interchangeable heads, or at least with a hard and a soft face. This hammer, or mallet, is invaluable for dismantling items which would bruise if hit with a steel hammer. For example, it will undo chromium-plated wing nuts without marking them, and a larger version will hammer out a car bodywork without further marking the metal.

Surveyor's tape

This is a really long tape which comes into its own when checking large measurements or marking out for paths and patios.

Grindstone

This is useful for re-sharpening steel chisels or removing damaged metal on edge tools prior to re-sharpening on a stone. You would be wise to wear safety glasses when using the grindstone.

Tools for specific jobs

Once you start, the collection of tools seems endless, and you will add items needed for specific jobs.

A ***bottled gas blowtorch*** is useful for paint removal, soldering and light brazing work. This is easier to use than the old blow-lamp which needed priming and heating before it would light. Nowadays you can get the added refinement of automatic crystal ignition. This is useful when working outside on ladders or scaffolding as it means ignition is a one-handed job.

If you tackle metalwork, such as wrought iron work or car body repairs, a simple ***welding outfit*** will be an invaluable addition to the kit. This can be mains operated, or for smaller jobs, battery-operated.

Where rusted nuts and bolts are encountered, a ***nut splitter*** is useful. This has a wedge which can be tightened against the face of a nut until it cuts through to the thread, making it possible to lift the nut away.

Some of the attachments available for a power tool

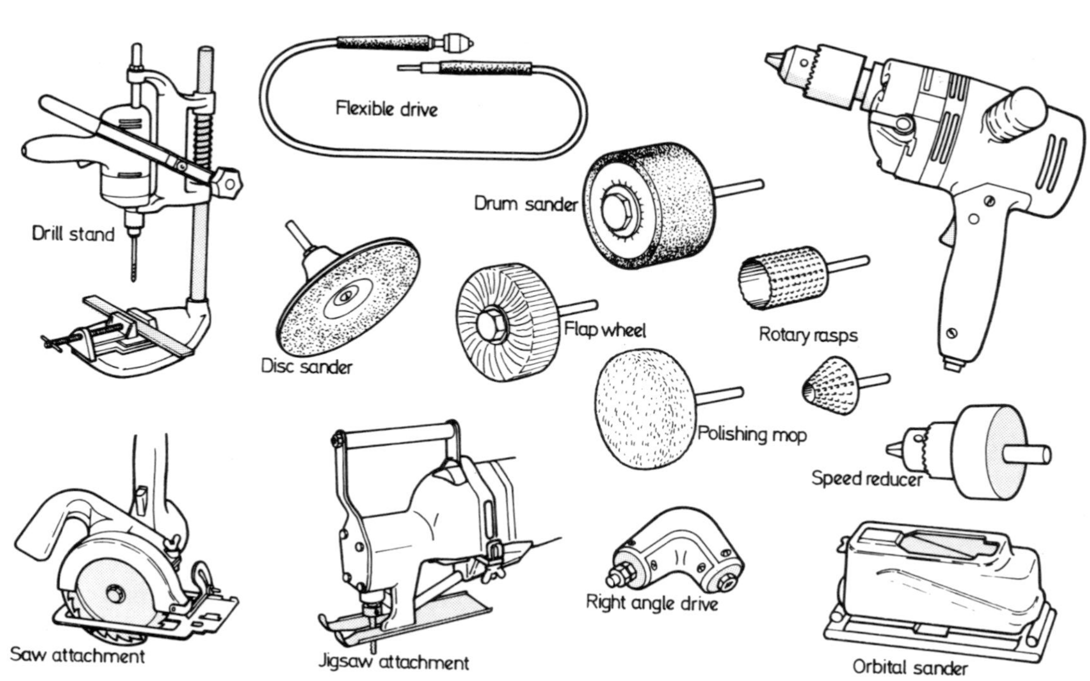

Stud rivet kits are useful for many repair jobs. The riveter rather resembles a pair of pliers into which is fed a special hollow rivet. Pressure on the handles expands the rivet until a special pin breaks away, leaving a neat repair.

A *case opener* is a tough metal lever with a shaped end which is used for opening packing cases. It is ideal for lifting stubborn floorboard nails and for levering up boards when access below is required.

Power tools

So far, we have reviewed a considerable number of hand tools, and while it is possible to get by with just these, the introduction of power tools will help considerably. It will take the hard work out of many jobs; speed up your work very noticeably and, in many cases, produce far more accurate work.

It is worth a little thought before investing in power tool equipment, for there are two approaches to the subject. First, you can buy a basic power tool to which you plan to affix various attachments made for that tool. Or second, you can buy a power tool for drilling, then buy individually powered tools designed to do specific jobs.

The first approach is the cheapest, but you will be limited because a drill has not the ideal speed for actions such as sawing. You may find that the way you hold the tool has to be a compromise because the attachment protrudes from the chuck of the drill. There is also the disadvantage that you may be for ever changing attachments—though work can often be planned to change as little as possible.

The second approach is the most expensive, but it has the advantage that each tool is designed for a specific job, and that it is ready for use whenever you pick it up. There is a trend towards integral units—certainly as a person gains experience—and has the money for the investment.

Power drills

You will find these come in a wide price range, from a small single speed unit designed basically for drilling, through to a powerful variable speed model incorporating hammer action. The variable speed is useful as it enables you to make a slow, deliberate start when drilling items like ceramic tiles or glass, increasing speed as the drill tip bites. You can also adjust from slow for drilling to fast for sawing and fine sanding.

Hammer action is invaluable when drilling in tough surfaces like dense paving slabs and reinforced concrete lintels. When hammering, special masonry drills should be used.

Sanding

The most common attachment is the disc sander, which fits into the chuck of a power drill. It should only be used for coarse working as the circular action tends to make score marks which are difficult to lose. Various grades of abrasive are available, from coarse to fine.

The more effective tool is the drum sander. This again fits in the chuck, but it has a drum of foam around which is fitted a belt of abrasive. Belts are available from very fine to coarse, and they are held in place by a heat-softened wax. Because the rotation is in one direction, it can be worked with the grain of a piece of wood, making no scratch marks. Also, because of its size, the drum is self-cooling, which means the abrasive is less likely to clog with melted paint when sanding down painted surfaces.

The latest addition to the range of sanders is the flap wheel. This is made up of strips of abrasive mounted on a central core. Flap wheels come in a range of sizes, and are effective for work like reducing rust or smoothing awkward sections of timber.

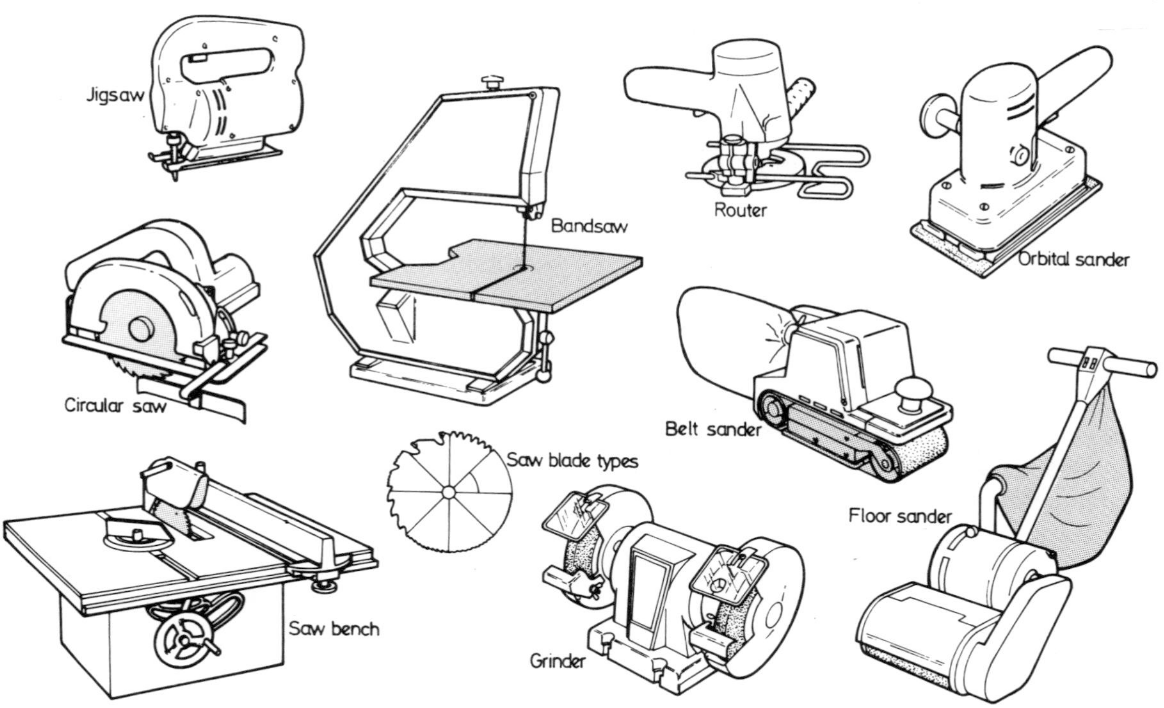

Integral motor power tools—designed to do one job efficiently

For fine surface finishing over large areas the orbital sander is useful. This is best bought as an integral power unit, and if you watch it closely you will see it makes very fine circular passes—so fine that the wood is not marked.

For larger jobs where a lot of sanding is to be done, you can get a belt sander, and for even larger projects such as floor resurfacing there is a belt floor sander with vacuum cleaner action for collecting the dust. The two latter sanders are best hired when required.

Sawing

Attachments are available for fitting to many power tools, but the depth of cut and the actual cutting power is limited. Sawing is also a two-handed operation. One hand for the power tool and the other for the handle of the saw attachment. For regular cutting work the integral saw is a good investment. It cuts at the right speed; is balanced for one-hand operation, and gives a greater depth of cut. Various circular saw blades are available, and the illustration shows the main tooth forms. Say what the blade is for when buying. Such blades must be sharp if they are to cut without imposing a strain on the power source.

Apart from straight cutting, you can cut curves and awkward shapes with a jig saw. This is available as an attachment or as an integral unit, and it does take a little practice to be able to cut to a line without wavering.

For those wishing to do considerable cutting to shape, and wishing to tackle thicker materials, there is the more expensive bandsaw. Here, the saw blade is in a continuous strip, turning in one direction.

Where finer control is required when cutting, the ideal is to use a saw bench.

Here the blade is set below the work, protruding through it, and the work is fed to the blade. It is vital that great care is taken to keep the hands away from the blade, and the guard fitted should be used at all times. The simplest table will be set at right angles to the blade, but a useful refinement is to have a tilting table so that angled cuts can be made to a very fine wheel setting.

I would include with the cutting tools the now well established abrasive cutting discs which will cut through materials as varied as brickwork and corrugated iron sheeting. Very great care must be used with such discs. No guard is used, yet the disc will cut more rapidly than a circular saw blade. Wear safety glasses to protect your eyes from flying particles.

Just a few of the tools it would pay you to hire rather than buy. These will only be needed occasionally for specific jobs and it is not worth buying your own. Remember to contact the hire shop in good time as these large tools are in great demand. Especially in the summer!

Routing

The router is a more specialised shaping and cutting tool running at very high speeds and using specially shaped cutting heads for different jobs. This is an integral tool because of the high speed, and it is useful for reproducing mouldings, edgings, rebates and other shapes not easily produced in any other way.

The router may be a hand-held tool offered to the job, or it may be bench-mounted and the work offered to it.

Drilling

Apart from normal hand-held drilling operations, a vertical drill stand which holds a drill firmly in place is ideal for fine drilling work—such as repairs to metalwork or dowel hole drilling. The base may be fixed at right angles to the drill, or tilted to a given angle.

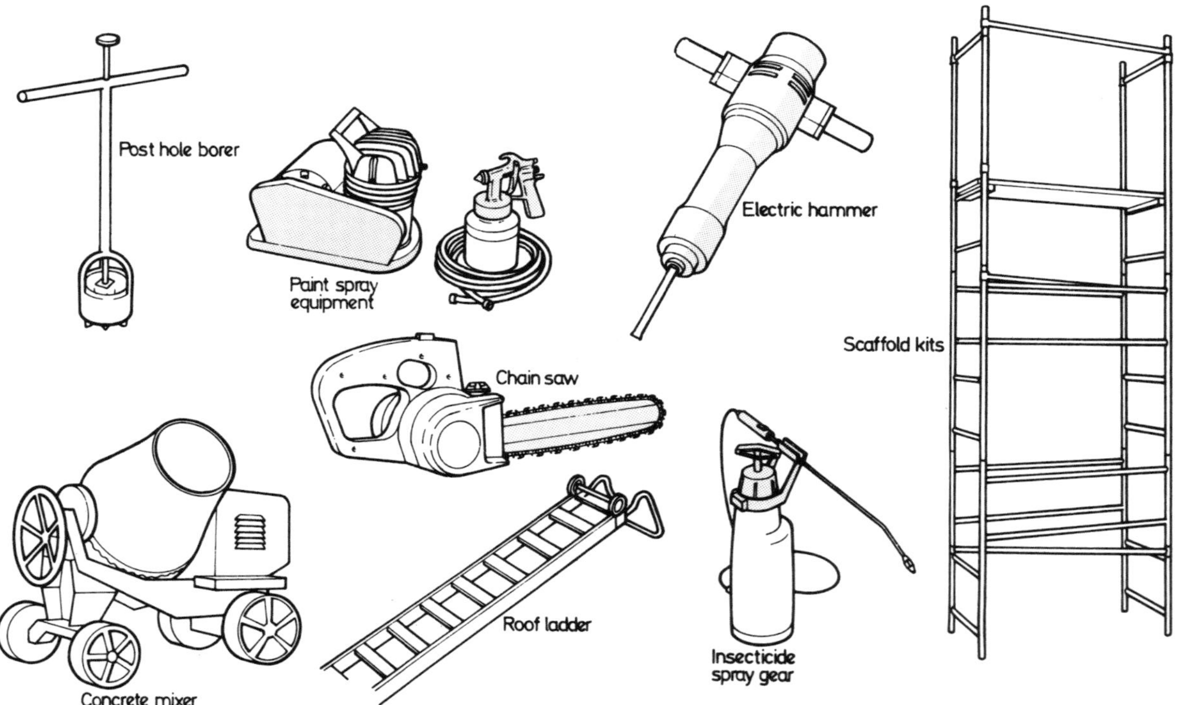

Spray painting

Attachments are available for some power tools to convert the drill into a spray gun, but the best guns are again integral units with a powered feed. This may take the form of air pressure which forces the paint from a nozzle, or it may be pumped liquid forced through the nozzle. The latter is the most effective method of painting as there is far less movement of air-borne spray. Even so, it is wise to mask all areas nearby which are not to be painted. Use masking tape, not clear adhesive tape. With small items, make a booth of cardboard to contain any over-spray.

Rotary rasps

These have the same action as the router, except they are coarser in action. A set of rasps which will fit in the chuck of a power tool are a useful addition to the kit for shaping and boring.

Flexible drive

This is a means of transmitting the rotary action of the drill through a flexible cable to a secondary chuck; it can be very useful for fine drilling and shaping work in awkward spots. Care should be taken not to overload the cable.

Speed reducer

If you have a power tool with a set speed, it is possible to buy a speed reducer designed to fit into the chuck of the tool. By holding the knurled wheel, considerable reduction in speed can be obtained, making the tool more suited to starting a drill tip on smooth surfaces such as tile or metal.

Right-angle drive

A special angle attachment is available which turns the drive from a power tool chuck through 90° to a secondary chuck. This device is very useful when working in confined spaces or up against a wall, such as when drilling holes for new plumbing pipes as close to a corner as possible.

Tool hire

As mentioned earlier, there will be occasions when specialist equipment would be of assistance, yet it is not worth buying it outright. This is where a good hire shop will prove extremely useful. Just about every professional tool is available on loan, including chain saws, electric and petrol concrete mixers, pneumatic drills, steam wallpaper strippers, rotary cultivators, scaffold kits, woodworm treatment sprays and ancillary equipment, extra ladders and scaffold boards, paint spray guns and industrial size power tool equipment.

Delivery and collection by your own transport will save on costs, as will careful planning of work so that you do not keep hired items any longer than necessary.

Find your local hire shop and get a catalogue. This will show you the range of gear available, and the current prices for hire either by the day or the week.

Access equipment

Apart from the tools listed, it is vital that you have the correct means of reaching your work, whether it be just to the ceiling or up to the roof ridge. Never take chances on make-do equipment!

For interior work you need a sturdy pair of steps with wide base and preferably a grip handle at the top so that you have a grip to steady yourself. Make sure you have non-slip treads.

For exterior jobs, an extension ladder is necessary. It should extend at least three rungs above gutter level at the highest wall height, have comfortable treads and be easy to handle. You have a choice of timber or alloy, both now being similar in price. The alloy will last longest without signs of deterioration, but timber is much warmer on the hands in really cold weather. Metal also tends to get grubbier than wood, but it is considerably lighter. The choice is yours!

This is the correct way to raise a ladder. This way you will not lose control over it

Cord-operation to raise a ladder section is useful, but unless you are experienced, it pays to have help when raising and lowering. The illustration shows the safe way of raising an extending ladder. Where a three-section ladder is needed, you definitely need help, for when extended such a ladder can be very difficult to control.

Where you need to reach the roof ridge or a chimney stack, it is wise to hire a roof ladder which hooks securely over the ridge. The wheels are so you can get the ladder in place easily—then you merely turn the ladder over.

Where walls are to be repaired or painted a scaffold kit designed specially for d-i-y use is invaluable. This comes in easy-to-assemble sections, and once erected to the required height provides a safe, comfortable working platform. The tower should always be climbed from the inside to avoid tipping. If such a tower proves too much of a financial outlay, you can hire one. But plan your work carefully so you do not keep it too long. Modest charges soon add up.

An alternative working platform can be made using two ladders, a pair of builder's cripples and scaffold boards. The cripples are supports on to which the boards can be laid to provide a walkway. A simple guard rail will make working that much safer. This can be behind you just below waist height.

Chapter 2 Materials for repairs

The range of materials now available for d-i-y use is now quite bewildering, and the difficulty nowadays is not finding a remedy, but of knowing out of the scores of types available which is best suited to the job in hand. Whatever the material, it must be stressed at the outset that new material must go on to clean, dry, firm surfaces. You cannot expect even the best filler to grip loose rust, flaking paint or rotting wood.

Basic materials and how to deal with them will be covered in following chapters, so for the time being we will have a look at some of the products at your disposal and their applications.

Fillers

Papier mâché

I make no excuse for starting with probably the oldest and best tried filler whose history, I would guess, goes back thousands of years. It is made by shredding newspaper, adding water to thoroughly soften it, squeezing out, then adding a quantity of glue size powder dissolved in water. Mix to the consistency of putty, and it becomes a good filler for stopping gaps in floorboards. It will set hard in time and can be sanded down as necessary.

To match stained boards, merely add water stain, a little at a time, until you get the right colour. The material is also extremely cheap to produce!

Cellulose filler

This is of far more recent origin and the cellulose filler has proved invaluable for sealing cracks in plaster and wood. Because of its adhesive nature, it does not shrink out of a crack like the old fillers, and, once set, it can be sanded, scraped or drilled.

Plaster fillers

A number of plaster-based materials are still available, and if bought in bulk they can prove cheaper to use for the larger repair jobs. One of the most useful materials is Keenes cement, which is cheap and easy to use. It does set quite fast, so only small

Mastics are available in a number of forms. Here are some of them. Right, to add adhesion to a mix, use pva adhesive in the mixing water

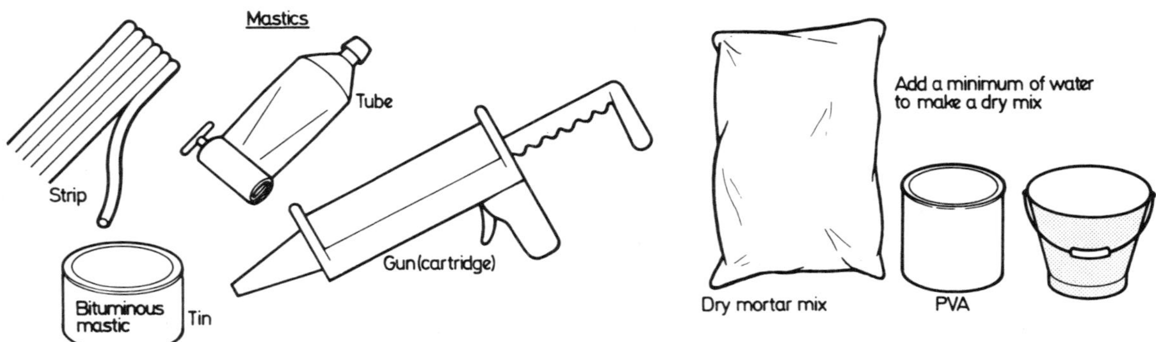

amounts should be mixed at a time. Deep holes should be filled in a number of layers rather than in one go, and the minimum of water should be added.

Plaster of Paris is not really suitable for d-i-y use because it goes off far too quickly. It could be used as a deep gap filler for filling the hole three quarters full, as it will set almost immediately. You could then finish off with cellulose or Keenes cement with no delay.

Swedish putty

This is another old but effective way of repairing or filling where a water-resistant surface is required. Cellulose filler is made up with water in the normal way but keeping the mix very dry, then a quantity of oil-based paint is added and worked in until a creamy mix is produced. It is ideal for sealing gaps behind areas like old stoneware sinks where there is no expansion and contraction movement.

Fine surface filler

Another relative newcomer, sometimes called spachtel, this is supplied as a ready-mixed paste. It has a very fine finish, and is ideal for filling cracks in timber prior to painting. It is supplied either in tubs or in plastic tubes. The tubed material lasts better because the air cannot get at the filler.

Stoppings

These are well-established products well known by woodworkers as first-rate fillers. Smooth in texture and adhesive by nature they fill without cracking away as they dry. A number of colours are available to match major timbers, making them suitable for filling timbers which are then to be finished with varnish or seal. You can also buy an exterior grade for use out of doors.

Most fillers are affected by damp, so for items like filling cracks in garden furniture, use an exterior filler. Like the fine surface fillers, stopping comes ready-mixed.

Putty

One of the traditional fillers and sealers, putty still may be used as long as it is well protected by paint. It will harden as it dries, so it is not suitable for areas where there is likely to be movement, as it merely cracks away, leaving a gap into which damp can seep.

Remember there are two types. Standard linseed oil putty, which dries by the absorption of the oils into the wood, and metal casement putty which will dry even though the metal to which it adheres is non-porous. Be sure you specify which is needed when tackling window repairs.

Mastics

These may resemble putty, but they have the advantage of remaining flexible even after the surface has dried. This is a big advantage when dealing with materials which may move, if only slightly—for example, when sealing a gap between brick and a timber frame.

Mastic comes in a number of forms. One type takes the form of thin strips rather resembling rolled Plasticine, ready to be pressed into small gaps. It is also available in tubes to be dispensed rather like toothpaste, and in cartons which fit in a special mastic gun. The gun is ideal for larger sealing jobs, and the tube nozzle can be cut to whatever diameter is required.

A bituminous mastic is also available, usually supplied in a tin, and this is ideal for sealing gaps in bituminous roofing sheets or for filling cracks in rainwater goods. Added strength can be achieved by working hessian strip into the repair, then laying bitumen over it. This helps particularly where there may be slight movement, likely to open up a repaired joint.

Mortar mix

Cement-based mortar consisting of sand and cement is suitable for repairing cracks in concrete, but it needs to be reinforced by the addition of pva adhesive. This can be added to the water used to make up the mortar, and it can also be brushed liberally into cracks and gaps, using the adhesive neat, prior to applying mortar. If you do not add the adhesive, the mortar will tend to crack away unless laid very thick.

You can buy the ingredients to make your own mortar or, for smaller projects, you can buy dry mixes at the builders merchants. All you need do is add water. If you do not finish a bag, seal it in a polythene bag and store in a dry place or the whole lot will go off.

Screeding compound

This is more than a gap filler. It is a resurfacing material and can be used for levelling uneven concrete floors prior to putting down floorcovering. When mixed to the right consistency, it pours rather like syrup, finding its own level. This saves the skilled operation of trowelling out to get a smooth surface that used to be necessary.

Read the instructions carefully so you do not mix more than can be used in a stipulated time. All cement-based materials go off quicker in warm weather.

Two-part fillers

Epoxy resin fillers are now very well established, particularly for car body repair work, though they can be used for many repairs such as sealing cracks in guttering or building up sections of damaged metalwork.

The filler is usually grey in colour and it consists of two parts. When mixed at the recommended quantities, the filler immediately starts to harden by chemical action—and nothing will stop it, even if the material is submerged in water. For this reason it is important to mix only enough for the job in hand, or you can end up with a lot of waste which cannot be re-softened.

With large gaps, it is wise to reinforce the repair with wire gauge or perforated zinc over which the filler is spread. Alternatively, the filler can be reinforced with glass fibre

The simple way to level an uneven solid floor

How to use an epoxy-based repair material

bandage built up sandwich-fashion and then coated with filler, working it well into the bandage.

Ceramic putty

Another material closely related to the epoxy filler is an epoxy putty. Here, a material closely resembling putty is supplied in two parts. Both parts remain reasonably soft and pliable until equal parts are mixed together, after which the material sets rock hard. Once set, it is impervious to water, grease and most chemicals.

Ceramic putty is ideal for repairs to sanitary ware, sealing gaps, encasing wires. It is best kept for smallish jobs as epoxies tend to be on the expensive side for large projects.

Sealants

A tubed sealant based upon silicone rubber is now available to be used mainly as a gap sealer. Designed to be squeezed from a nozzle, it becomes tough-dry in a matter of minutes, setting to a rubbery yet flexible consistency which maintains its high adhesion even in damp conditions.

There is a real art in spreading it—pushing forward, nozzle first. Read the instructions carefully and do a test run before tackling anything too ambitious!

Adhesives

Nothing in the d-i-y field has changed more than the range of adhesives. From a basic one or two types we now have a vast

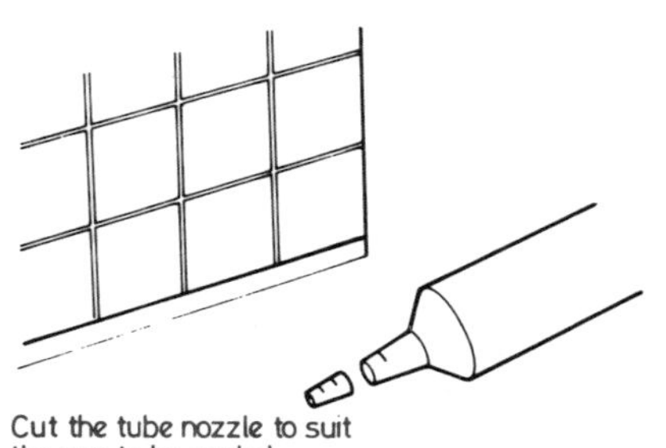

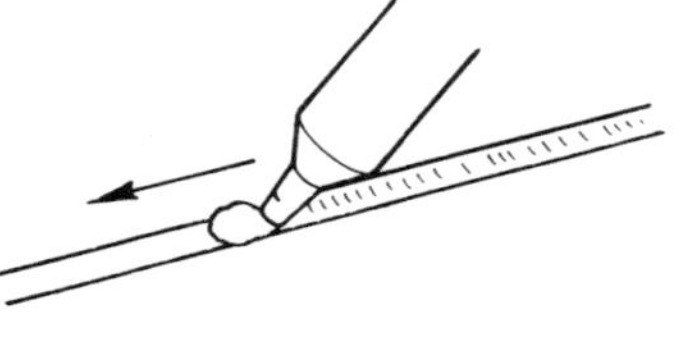

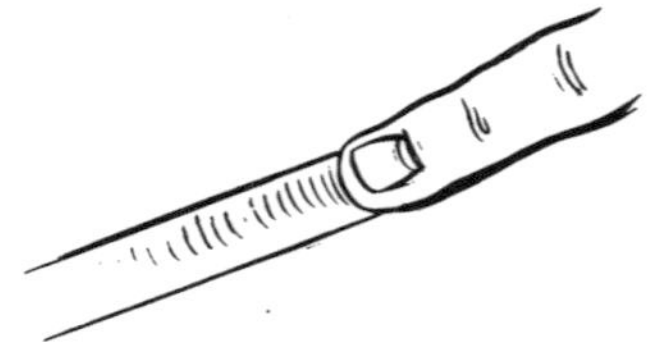

Using a sealant to fill a gap such as is found between a tiled wall and a bath

number, and I think it fair to say that there is not one which will deal with all materials. Each type has its advantages and limitations, so it is wise to read very carefully any pack or packet before buying. Here are the most common ones you will encounter.

Animal glue

This is the good old Seccotine or Croid-type material which served us so faithfully over the years. It is still around in tubes, and it has a place for simple repairs where the wood can be held while the adhesive sets; where slight staining does not matter, and where no damp is likely to be present. It has no real advantages over more modern materials.

Resin adhesive

This is usually supplied as a powder designed to be mixed with water as required, and is resistant to damp, making it suitable for exterior repairs. It is a strong, reliable woodworking adhesive.

PVA adhesive

Supplied as a liquid with the consistency and appearance of single cream, this is one of the most versatile adhesives introduced in recent years. It gives strong joints, is resistant to damp and it keeps well.

It has many applications—from the ideal card adhesive for the nursery to woodworking. It can be used as an additive for concrete to increase its general adhesion and it can be used as a surface coating for concrete to stop it dusting. You will also find it supplied for fixing expanded polystyrene wall veneers and ceiling tiles. Remember to buy it in the most economic way possible for the job in hand. A tub used for wall veneer fixing will keep a nursery school in adhesive for a whole term!

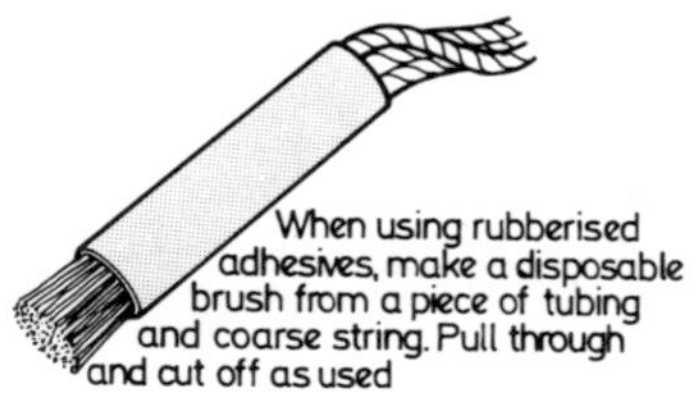

Rather than ruin good brushes, make your own which can be disposed of after use

Clear resin

This has become the most popular household adhesive for general repair work. It has a strong solvent which dries off quickly, so you get strong joints in a short time. Coat both surfaces, allow to go touch dry and then press together. It is best suited to flexible surfaces, and is not designed for woodworking joints.

Rubber resin

This is the popular impact type adhesive used widely for securing laminated plastics. It is applied to both surfaces, allowed to become touch-dry, then the two surfaces pressed together.

If the surface area is fairly large, it will secure timber to a flat surface such as plaster. I have fixed pelmet battens in place over plaster hiding a concrete lintel with complete success. It will fix most flexible materials, but is not really suitable for woodworking joints.

Latex

This rather resembles the rubber resin, but it is milky in colour with a strongish smell. It is designed for carpet and fabric binding and it gives a quick clean joint. Another advantage is that it rubs easily from the fingers—something you cannot do with rubber resin.

Epoxy resin

This is a two-part material, resin and hardener, and once equal parts have been mixed together, setting is by chemical action which nothing can stop. It is ideal for repairs to metal, china and glass, and, once set, being unaffected by heat, damp or most chemicals.

Two basic types are now available. A standard adhesive which sets over some 12 hours, faster if the material is warmed, and a fast setting adhesive which is set in about 5 minutes. The latter is extremely useful where it is hard to hold pieces in place while the adhesive sets. In extreme circumstances it is now possible to hold the pieces in place until the resin sets. Polythene gloves help here as some people are allergic to epoxy resins.

Cyanoacrylate

This is a most remarkable material which gives the benefits of almost instantaneous repairs to hard materials like metal and glass and flexible materials like synthetic rubbers. It resembles water to look at, but there the resemblance ends, for one small drop is all that is needed to give an immediate bond between surfaces. For this reason, extreme caution is called for. Take care not to get it on fingers or eyelids. It will stick these together with equal speed and is then very difficult indeed to get them unstuck! It is also expensive, so keep it for small jobs which need speed.

I have found it has the disadvantage that, because of the speed of setting, there is little time to position awkward pieces, say, of a broken vase or piece of pottery. If fitting together is tricky, use an epoxy resin material where you have more time.

PVC

For sticking pvc materials such as plastic raincoats, paddling pools and beach balls, you need special pvc adhesive which has a solvent content to soften and weld the pvc together. Some materials seem suitable, but when dry they can be peeled away because there has been no solvent

Using an epoxy resin adhesive for repair work

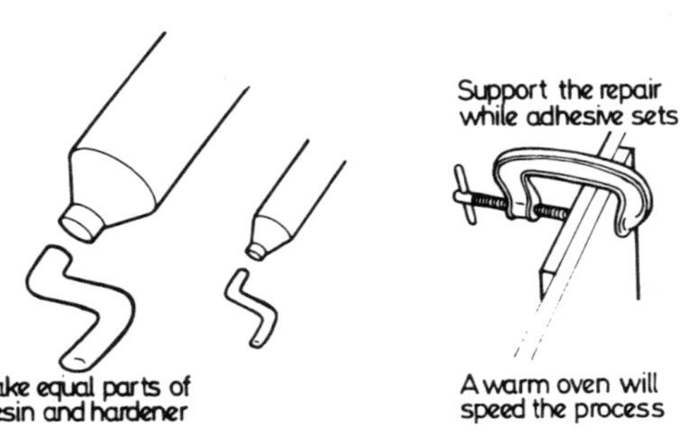

For awkward or rapid repairs, use a quick set adhesive -the repair could be held, as setting time is 5-10 minutes

action. When in doubt, experiment on a small area before tackling a major repair.

You can also buy a pvc repair tape which has the same action. This is useful for emergency repairs.

Polystyrene cement

This too has a solvent action, and is now widely used for model kits where the basic plastic used is polystyrene. As it has a solvent effect, keep surplus adhesive off the face of the plastic as it will mark it.

Choice of adhesive

Because of the complexity of materials available today—especially among the plastics—it may be necessary to find the right adhesive by experiment, perhaps because you cannot find out what the material is you wish to repair. Try your adhesion tests on scrap materials if possible, and make sure the joint is really dry before testing for adhesion.

Problem areas include expanded polystyrene. Do not use adhesive with a heavy solvent—such as rubber resin. It will completely dissolve the plastic. Do not try to stick polythene; it has a wax-like surface which rejects all known adhesives. Polythene will have to be heat-welded. Nylon has the same nature and I know of no adhesive which will hold it.

Do not use hard-setting materials like resin adhesives on flexible surfaces; they will crack up when flexed. The reverse also applies. Do not use flexible adhesives such as rubber resins on small joint areas where strain may be applied; the flexible adhesive will not take the strain.

Tapes

Adhesives are being backed up by a whole range of adhesive tapes which very often simplify a job. Double-sided adhesive pads can be used for fixing metal tiles to walls, and bathroom fittings and hooks to walls or doors. Double-sided tapes can be used for securing floorcoverings of all kinds, and heavier duty adhesive pads are now used for holding wall panelling to a wall.

As with all fixing jobs, it is important that the surfaces to be fixed are clean, dry and free from grease. Carpet tape will prevent carpet fraying at the edges. pvc tape will repair rips in pvc items, masking adhesive tape will protect areas you do not wish to paint, and insulating tape will protect electrical wiring.

Nails

You are sure to need nails at some time, so it pays to keep a good selection, classified according to size and shape. Here are the most common ones together with a rough guide as to their use.

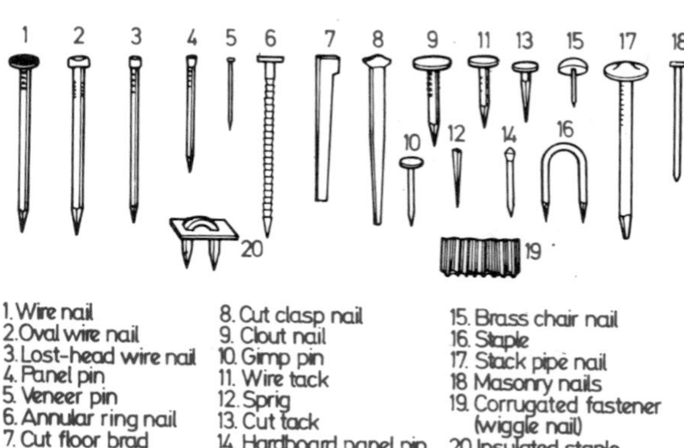

Make sure you choose the right nail for the job. There are plenty to choose from

Bear in mind that it is possible to get rust-resistant nails, and these should be used wherever there is the chance of rusting. The traditional rustless nail was galvanised, and this is still quite adequate for many exterior jobs. But you can also get aluminium alloy nails which have a far smoother finish. I would choose these wherever possible.

Wire nail

This is the common round nail with a flat head, useful for all framing jobs where fairly large sections of softwood are being used. If the round nail has to be used in thin section timber or with hardwoods, always drill a hole to prevent the wood splitting.

Oval wire nail

As the name suggests, the body is oval, making it less prone to splitting wood. Use it with its narrowest profile along the wood grain. You will see it has a different shape head too, which makes it possible to sink the head below the wood surface. A nail punch can be used to do this, after which the remaining small hole can be filled.

Lost head wire nail

This is the nail to use for carpentry repair work. It makes a smaller hole; is far less likely to split the wood, and its head is designed to be sunk below the surface of the wood.

The remaining hole can then be filled.

When used with hardwood, it is still wise to drill holes first to prevent the nail splitting the wood.

Panel pin

You will find these useful for cabinet and furniture repairs—especially for securing moulding. The fine body will not split the wood, and the head will sink easily below the surface.

Veneer pin

Not such a common item these days, but if you have to make repairs to veneered surfaces, they are designed to hold veneer in place while your glue sets—then they are pulled out.

Ring nail

The serrated body of this nail drives home easily enough, but it resists being drawn. This makes it ideal for holding materials firm where a normal nail might slip. For example, it will hold hardboard to a timber floor when there is slight spring in the floor. Also, it will hold firm in woods like red cedar where normal nails can often be drawn with the fingers, the wood is so soft.

Cut floor brad

This is the crudest form of nail, being cut from sheet metal. Its rough rectangular form affords a very good grip, and you will find it used in house construction for jobs like securing floorboards.

Cut clasp nail

Another nail cut from sheet metal and used in building for rough joinery work where a good grip is needed. This nail was also widely used for fixing into masonry before the hardened masonry nail became available.

Clout nail

This has a short body and large head, designed for holding sheet materials such as roofing felt. Serrations on the nail body help to give it a better grip in timber. Choose galvanised nails for all exterior work.

Gimp pin

With a square body and flat head, this nail is designed for holding material to a framework in upholstering.

Wire tack

This has a shorter body and larger head than the gimp pin, and this also is used in upholstering, mainly where frame sections are thicker.

Sprig

A very useful little headless tack with a sharp point. It is used for holding glass in place prior to applying putty to a timber frame. Also useful for holding glass, picture and backing in place when picture framing.

Cut tack

This tack has a large head and a heavily tapered body, making it easy to drive and to withdraw. It is used for securing materials such as underfelt and upholstery fabric to timber.

Panel pin

The type shown is called a deep drive pin, as the diamond-shape head is automatically driven below the surface as it is hammered home. It is ideal for fixing plywood and hardboard where the heads are to be hidden with filler. Because of the head shape, panel pins are a little harder to hit with a hammer! Shanks may be round or square.

Chair nails

Usually brass, chair nails resemble a drawing pin with domed head. You will need them for upholstery repairs, for holding the covering fabric in place. They may also be used to disguise tack heads and also as a decorative finish.

Staples

You will find these in upholstered furniture, holding the springs in place. They are also widely used for fencing, wherever wire or netting has to be held.

Insulated staples

Used for holding electrical wiring in place, insulated staples usually comprise a square section staple with a small piece of insulating material at the head. This prevents the staple cutting into the wire or cable.

Stack pipe nails

You will not encounter many of these, but they are used for securing pipe brackets to masonry. The large head is designed to sit neatly on the bracket.

Masonry nails

These are especially hardened nails designed to be driven straight into masonry to hold battening in place. Check on the recommended sizes for given types, for it is important that not too much nail is driven into the masonry. A long nail will merely act as a metal wedge, splitting a brick or block, and giving no grip at all.

Corrugated fasteners

These are useful for securing frame sections prior to covering with plywood or hardboard, and for joining boards together. The fastener pulls the two components together as it is driven home. Sometimes called wiggle nails.

Screws

Although a seemingly simple device, the screw is a most misunderstood piece of hardware. Through abuse and mis-use, simple fixing jobs become sheer hard work. The most important lesson to learn is that the holding power of a screw does not depend on the force used to drive it. In fact too much force can split wood or turn the head off the screw. The secret is to make start holes into which a screw can be driven with the minimum of force. Work is easier, and the holding power is in no way affected.

The illustration shows the holes you need to make. First, a clearance hole in the item to be fixed into which the shank of the screw just fits. Second, if the head of the screw is designed to be flush with the surface, you need a countersunk hole into which the head will recess. Third, you need a smaller diameter hole in the lower piece of wood into which the thread will not quite go, so it bites into the surrounding timber. A little grease or Vaseline on the screw thread will make driving even easier, and it will ensure that the screw comes out easily should it ever be necessary.

Screws are sold by gauge sizes—Number 8 or number 10. This refers to the diameter of the screw shank and it is calculated by measuring across the head in $^1/_{16}$ ths, doubling this figure and subtracting two. So, if the head measures $^5/_{16}$ in, doubling gives you 10; minus 2 equals 8. You have a number 8 screw. All you then need add is the length, so you would order a 2 in. number 8.

You will find that head shapes vary, but the most common are described below.

Countersunk screws

Here the head is designed to be recessed so that it ends up flush with the surface—or it could be taken lower and the remaining recess filled.

Raised countersunk screws

The head is recessed into the wood, but a slight dome remains proud of the surface.

Round head screws

The screw sits on the surface, and is the type which would be used in conjunction with washers, or to hold metal brackets in place.

Slot types

You will encounter three slot types which were mentioned earlier in this chapter under screwdrivers. These are:

Single slot. This is the traditional slot into which a standard screwdriver fits, and it is important that the driver chosen fits the screw head correctly. Too large a screwdriver will mean the tip slips from the slot. Too small a driver will twist the screwdriver blade.

Phillips cross slot. The cross has a simple cross section into which fits the tip of a special Phillips screwdriver. The big advantage is that the tip can't slip from the slot—an important point when screwing into a decorative surface.

Pozidriv slot. This is a more sophisticated cross slot where a specially shaped screwdriver tip fits so well into the slot that you can in fact pick up the screws on the tip. This is useful for starting screws in awkward to get at spots, and again you have the advantage that the driver does not slip out. Pozidriv screws come in a wide range of sizes, and it is essential to ensure that the screwdriver fits the head perfectly.

A relatively new screw design is available called the Twinfast. This has a special double thread which allows a screw to be driven much faster than normal.

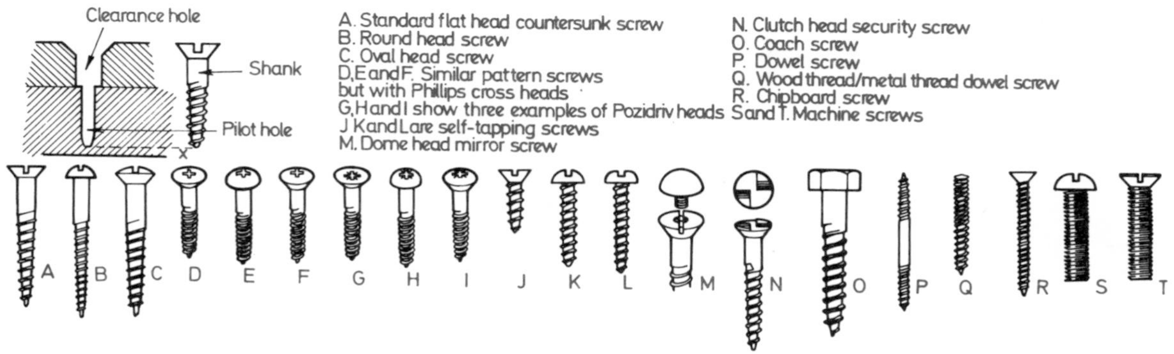

These are the most common screws you will encounter in repair work

Special screws

Apart from the normal range, there are all kinds of specials. Here are a few examples.

Chipboard screws

The shank and body of this screw are very similar in thickness so there is no wedge action when driving into chipboard. This helps prevent splitting. Even so it is wise to make start-holes to avoid splitting the board. Most chipboards split more readily than timber.

Self-tapping screws

Designed to be used for fixing metal sheet, they will drive into a prepared hole, cutting a way in for the thread to grip. They are widely used in cars for fixing items to the metalwork of the car. They are also used for cutting their own thread when driven into plastics. A start hole is necessary, then the thread cuts into the surrounding plastic.

Coach screws

A heavy screw with a head designed to be turned by spanner rather than screwdriver. Used for heavy woodworking.

Dome-head screws

Also called mirror screws, a special screw has a slot and a threaded hole into which a special dome head can be screwed after the screw is in place. This gives a decorative finish. There are now modern alternatives, including small plastic inserts which will press into the recess in a Pozidriv screw. Also, a dome and nylon collar which can be used press stud fashion when used in conjunction with dome head screws.

Machine screws

More of an engineering screw, this is designed to be used with threaded inserts or nuts. It is not designed to be driven into timber.

Clutch head screws

A special security screw which has an unusually designed head. There are faces upon which a screwdriver can bear to tighten the screw, but there are none for loosening the screw. Sloping surfaces deflect the screwdriver. Ideal for fixing padlock hasps and staples and any other item of hardware which you do not want anyone to interfere with.

While the standard screw is of steel, rust-resisting screws are available. Brass can be used for boatbuilding. Aluminium alloy can be used anywhere you are likely to encounter damp conditions which could cause corrosion.

Chapter 3 Timberwork

The first point to establish with timber is that it will not last for ever. In its natural state in the wood or forest, once a tree dies it starts to decay. It is attacked by the weather, many types of fungi, and wood boring insects until eventually the timber is broken down completely and absorbed into the soil.

When timber is used for construction work, you will find that the same processes will try to continue. If damp can get into it, it will rot and if left unprotected, it will be attacked by woodboring insects. Let us look at these enemies of timber in a little more detail.

Wet rot

This is quite a common form of rot, though it is the least serious as it will not spread from the area under attack. Timber has to be wet to start with, and the causes may range from rainwater gathering around the stump of a fence post, to an area of floorboards soaked by water leaking from a radiator or pipe.

Where do rot spores come from to start the infection? Well, the answer is that they are always in the air in vast quantities. For example a mushroom of 3 in diameter will produce in the region of 1,800 million spores. They are so small that they blow away in the wind, awaiting the day when they encounter damp wood on which they can start to grow.

Wet rot appears as whitish strands spreading over the timber surface; a rather dank and musty smell, and cracks running along the grain of the wood. It will also noticeably darken the wood.

When dealing with wet rot, the first step is to locate the source of dampness and stop it. As suggested above, this may mean draining a hole in which a post stands; repairing a leaking pipe joint or sealing a hole in a radiator. Whatever the cause, once the wood can start to dry out, the rot will die off. Unfortunately you may find that some of the timber has softened and decayed. This timber must be cut back to sound wood, then a new piece of wood inserted. It is a waste of time trying to patch up damaged wood with fillers. The immediate effect may look good, but soon the filler will work loose as it has nothing firm to hold on to.

Having made good the repair, treat the timber with a good wood preservative, putting it on generously, and if possible soaking the ends of timber sections in preservative. In locations where damp may

What to do if you encounter wet rot

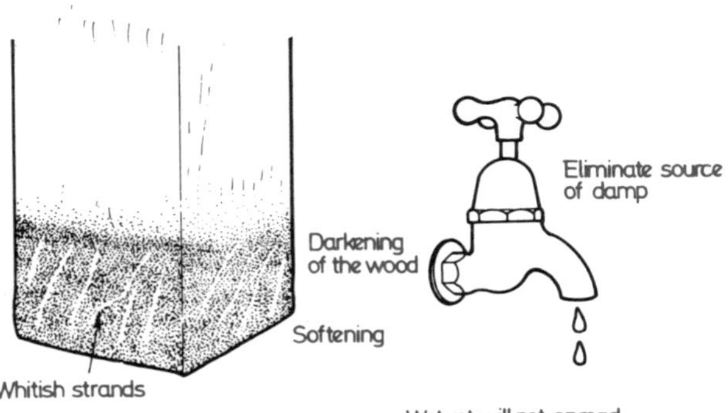

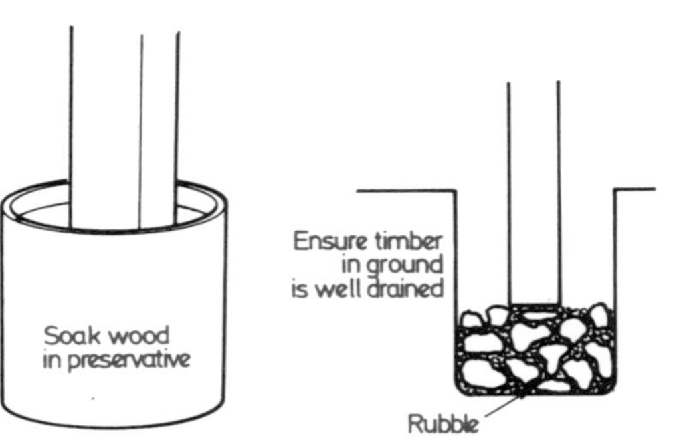

be encountered, it will pay you to buy pressure-impregnated timber for replacement work. It costs a little more than normal timber, and you can be sure that nothing will affect it. Alternatively, for fencing work, make up a single trough with bricks and heavy gauge polythene sheeting, pour in your preservative, then lay the timber in the preservative and leave it to soak. This has far more effect than brush coating.

When you come to erect fence posts, stand the base of each post on rubble before filling in. This will ensure good drainage and prevent water accumulating at the base.

Dry rot

The name here is misleading, because the dryness refers to the wood after it has been attacked. It too must be wet if an attack is to develop—but under different circumstances from wet rot.

If timber is dry, it will not be attacked, even though there may be millions of spores in the air. However, given poor ventilation, and a moisture content above 20% (25% is ideal) the dry rot spores can start to germinate. The attack may take place just about anywhere in a house where the right conditions prevail. These may be under a floor where the ventilation has been reduced or cut off, behind a skirting board, in a cupboard or under built-in units.

The first signs are a musty smell in the room and perhaps the warping or cracking of timber. You will see cracks across the wood, rather resembling the crazed effect you see on soil suffering drought. This is the effect of the fungus feeding off the cellulose in the timber, and it results in a severe weakening and softening of the wood. You will be able to push a knife point into the affected areas.

If you lift the affected wood, you will somewhere find what is called a fruiting body—a mushroom-like growth, probably surrounded by a whitish mass of strands rather resembling dirty cotton wool. From here on it gets nasty, for behind the thin strands come thicker ones capable of carrying water. These transfer water to dry areas of timber, thus ensuring that the rot can continue to spread. It is not unknown for an attack in a cellar to reach very quickly to the roof timbers—even passing through brickwork on the way!

Obviously this type of rot is a far greater threat than the wet rot as it is not contained within the original damp area. For this reason, if you do find an attack, deal with it as quickly as possible. If you do suspect an attack, but would like it verifying, call in one of the specialist companies who deal with timber preservation and have a free survey.

Treating dry rot

The first job, having located the dry rot fruit, is to cut away timber and plaster until the full area of attack has been exposed. It is vital not to miss anything, or you may have the rot continuing elsewhere.

Having ascertained the extent of the attack, deal with the cause of the damp. It could well be a leaking drain or gulley; air bricks covered with board to 'prevent draughts'; a defective damp proof course; missing or damaged roof tiles; gutters leaking water on to the wall, defective plumbing or leaking radiators. Unfortunately—unlike wet rot—when you have cured the trouble, the job is not finished. All infected timber must be cut out and burned, and all surrounding brickwork, plaster and timber treated with a powerful fungicide or dry rot fluid.

Masonry can be sterilised by playing a

How to recognise and deal with dry rot

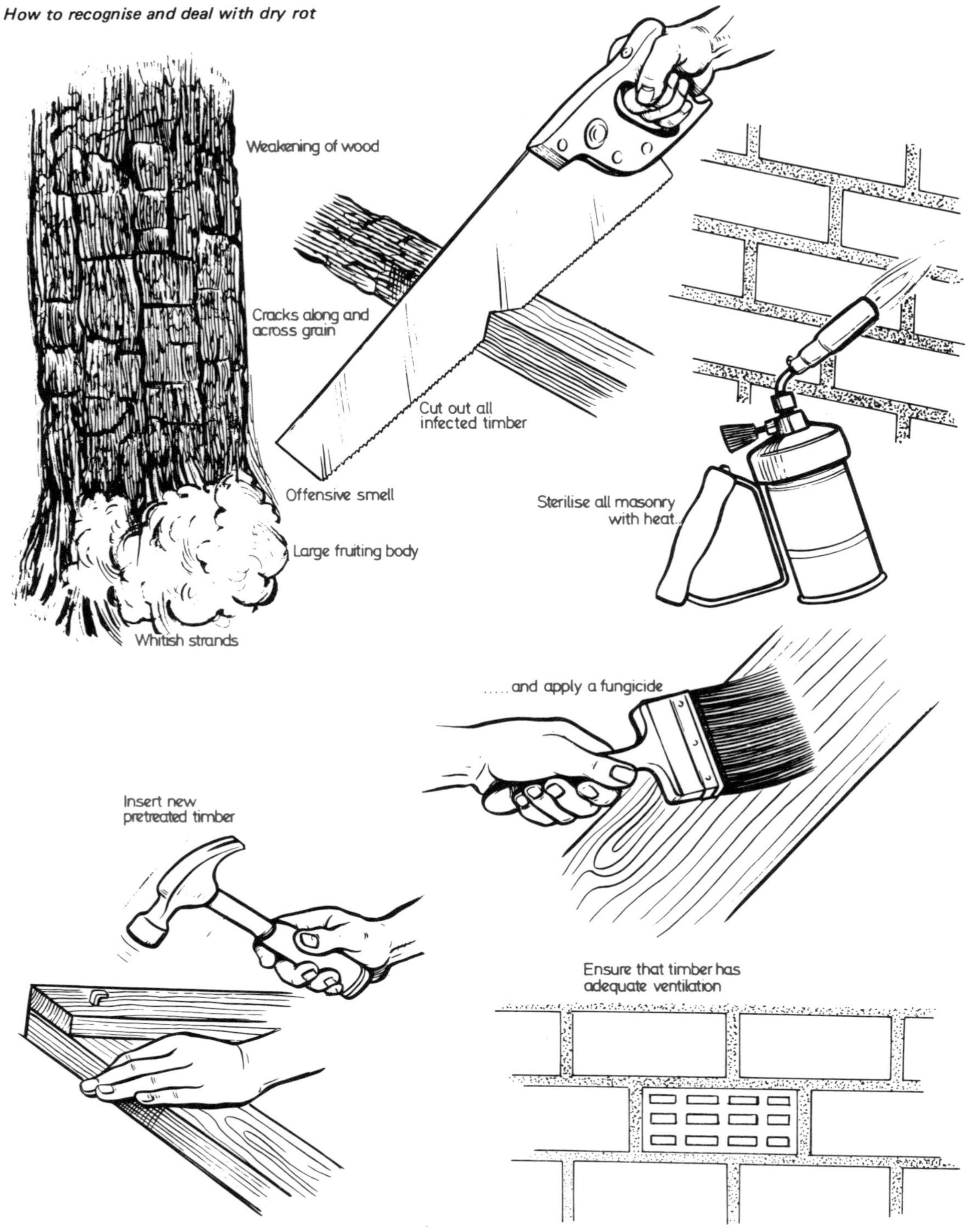

blowtorch over it, but great care must be taken not to start a fire.

Having cut out all infected wood, it should be replaced with either pre-treated timber, or with timber well soaked in preservative. It is far better to be over liberal with preservative – just in case an area should have been missed.

If you feel this job is too much for you, there are specialist companies who will do it, and offer a 20 or 30 year guarantee. This is certainly worth keeping against the day when you have to sell the property.

Of course it will cost considerably less to do the job yourself, but unfortunately there are still building societies who insist on the work being done by a specialist company before they will grant a mortgage. This is despite the fact that there are materials available to the d-i-y man which would do the job just as effectively.

With the repair work complete, make sure that the timber stays dry and well ventilated. Never block air bricks under the house. They are there to ensure adequate underfloor ventilation, and, as already stated, if the air is flowing freely, this keeps the moisture content low–and you will get no rot.

Insect attack

The beetle you are most likely to encounter is the common furniture beetle (or woodworm as it is better known). Its presence is usually detected by tiny holes in a piece of timber and a fine dust, which if you look very closely resembles tiny cigar-shaped pellets. Unfortunately, these are signs that your beetles have flown, for these are the holes they make as they leave the timber–so let us go back to the start of the life cycle.

A female beetle will lay from 20 to 40 eggs in crevices in rough timber, perhaps in the loft, or perhaps in the plywood backs of furniture. After about a month, the eggs hatch, and small grubs emerge which immediately start to burrow into the wood by eating it at one end and excreting it as pellets at the other. They continue tunnelling for about three years, after which each turns into a chrysalis; just under the surface of the wood. In four to eight weeks, it will turn into an adult beetle, and once the transformation is complete the beetle bites its way out of the wood, leaving behind that tell-tale little hole. The beetle will fly off to mate and then the whole cycle will be repeated.

I don't think the woodworm is really an insect to fear, for I have never heard of a house collapsing from its efforts. Even so, as soon as you discover an attack, it is wise to take steps to stop it. There are a number of ways you can do this, ranging from a simple local injection to large area timber treatment.

For a small area, you can get an aerosol can of fluid together with a tube and nozzle. Fit the tube to the can, insert the nozzle in a hole, and press. Protect your eyes against spray-back, and it pays to hold a cloth around the nozzle if you are near decorations, in case you splash them. Move from hole to hole injecting the fluid, and you can be assured that all the tunnels in that area will have been flooded, killing off any grubs inside, and making the wood unpleasant to eat.

For larger areas, the woodworm fluid can be brush applied, working it well into cracks and crevices where eggs are most likely to have been laid.

For difficult areas like loft spaces, you can hire a professional spray gun with lance and nozzle, and this will enable you to reach awkward places which are difficult to reach by hand. Use adequate fluid, but not too much. If you flood the area, you could have it soaking through your ceilings and making

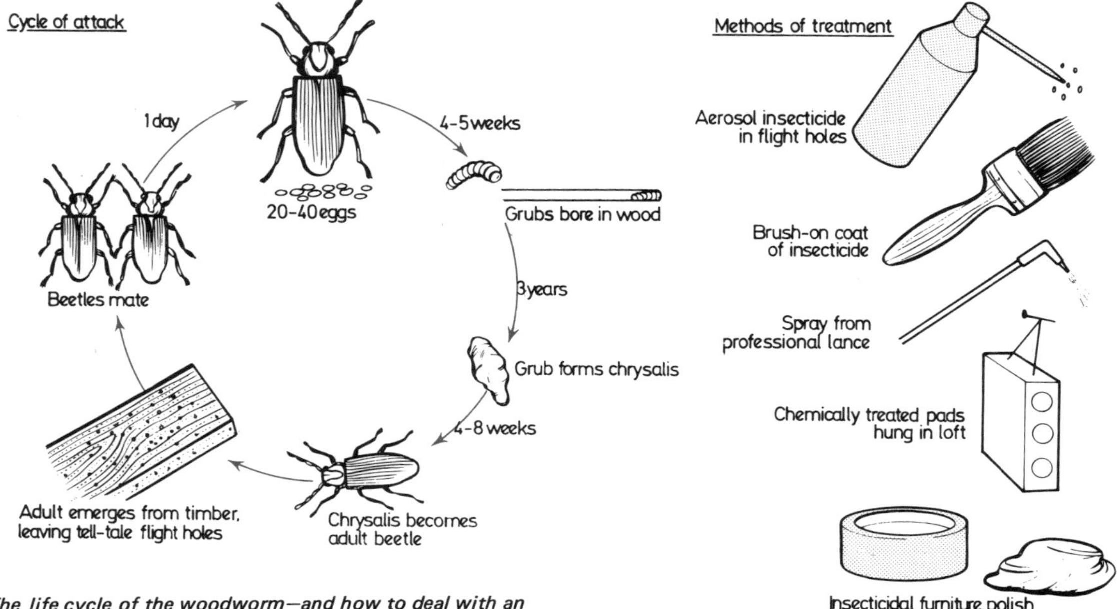

The life cycle of the woodworm—and how to deal with an attack

marks. It is also wise to hire an industrial face mask to keep the fumes away. I would also add safety glasses to keep spray away from the eyes.

This is another job where you can get a free professional survey if you have doubts about whether or not you have an attack. The company will either quote for doing the job, or for supplying you with the necessary materials to do it yourself. This is yet another area where some building societies insist the job is done by a specialist company before they will grant the loan. (Often hitting a young couple by giving them expense at a time they could well do without it!)

There are other beetles which cause trouble, but the only one which poses a serious threat in certain definable areas is the House Longhorn beetle. This really is a menace, because the beetle is 12—25 mm long (½—1 in) and it makes a hole up to 9 mm (3/8 in) across. It is found in roof timbers of attics where it attacks the softwood in a way which will in a very short time weaken the whole roof structure. Fortunately it is confined to the South of England, mainly in the west of Surrey. Should you find any largish holes with an elongated opening, filled with wood dust call in an expert company for a diagnosis. If it is the longhorn beetle, he must be dealt with quickly!

If you live in the area likely to be affected, make periodic checks in the loft for attack. Dig the point of a knife into structural timbers to see if there are tunnelways just below the surface.

The Death Watch beetle is not a domestic problem, although it is the bane of preservers of historic buildings where it will attack hardwoods which are old and damp. It practically never attacks sound, dry, ventilated timbers.

Apart from the action already described, it is possible to take precautionary measures to avoid beetle attack. One method is to buy special packs of chemical impregnated strips. A strip is hung in its container in the loft space, where fumes given off will kill off flying beetles. The strip needs renewing periodically, and details of the renewal times will be found on the pack.

Furniture may also be protected by using a special insecticidal furniture polish. The polish will contaminate cracks and gaps, killing off any beetles or eggs which come into contact with the timber. As has already been mentioned, the ideal protection is to use pre-treated timbers wherever new work is done, or replacement timbers are installed. Such timber, because it is pressure-impregnated, will be immune to insect attack throughout its life, and in view of the benefits, it is incredible to think that new housing is still constructed with un-treated timbers.

Exterior timbers also need protection, and you will find this dealt with in chapter 9. Now let us move to some other specific areas where timber may come under attack.

Doors which are painted

The front door is often affected in a number of ways, and because it is usually the first part of your house which greets the visitor it is worth keeping it looking good.

A timber panelled door which is painted may suffer from a breakdown of the paint film, and this is usually associated with slight shrinkage of the panelling—perhaps through excessive sun. This creates fine cracks in the paint film into which rain can get, and this will soak into the timber and eventually push off the paint.

The remedy is to attend to the door when it is really dry. Strip off the paint with a blowtorch, rub smooth, then fill all cracks with a fine surface filler or a stopping. A chemical stripper is not ideal here, as both the liquid used, and the neutraliser can damp down the timber. Using a blow-torch will, if anything, dry the timber even further.

Be sure to prime the bare wood, working it well into crevices. If you encounter knots which have resin seeping from them, cover the area of the knot with a patent knotting to seal in the resin. Otherwise when the sun gets on the door, it may continue to exude resin, pushing off any new paint coating.

Paint may also be pushed off by blistering. This is often caused by paint being applied when the moisture content of the wood is

Weak spots in your defences where damp will attack

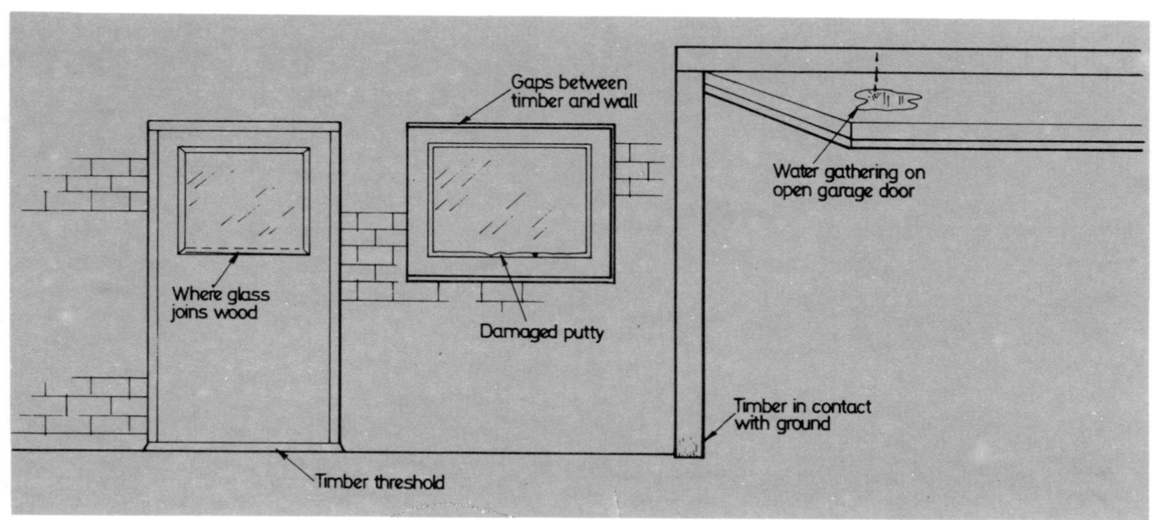

high. Moisture is trapped in and when the sun gets on the door, the moisture turns to vapour under sufficient pressure to push up the paint surface. The only remedy is to strip off the paint with a blowtorch and re-paint the wood when it is dry.

This is something to bear in mind when painting timber during the autumn and winter months. You will find that early and late in the day there may be condensation on the exterior of the house. Let this condensation dry off before painting.

Paint in sound condition may just have bleached out in the sun, making it look rather drab. Here, there is no need to strip it off, as it can form the foundation of a new coat. Rub the surface with a damp pumice stripping block to remove the glaze from the paint. This gives the surface a key ready for the new coat.

Wipe the surface clean with a lint-free rag and clean water, allow to dry, and the surface is ready for re-painting. If the colour is similar, you may get away with a straight coat of gloss paint, but bear in mind that a top coat has very little obliterative power; it resembles a coloured varnish. To hide a colour, you should use a matching undercoat which will obliterate, then follow this by the gloss coat.

Exposed front and back doors may be attacked by wet rot, particularly where a poor quality, badly seasoned timber has been used for a back door. On my quite modern estate, all the houses in our road suffered from rot in the back door after about nine years. This was caused by the reeded glass being inserted reed-side out, so that the retaining beading was not in close contact with the glass. In consequence, water could drain down into the door timber where it caused rotting.

The only remedy is to remove the glass, cut out all damaged timber and replace it with new, treated timber. Then re-glaze, making sure that the glass is well bedded into putty so there is no chance of water getting in. When you re-paint, take the new paint just on to the glass so you give a positive seal between putty and glass, or beading and glass.

Garage doors

A similar problem may be encountered with timber garage doors, where the part-glazing has weak points where moisture can get in. You will also get trouble with older tongue and groove panel doors where the wood has shrunk, forming cracks between panels and frames. Where there is the chance of slight movement, providing the wood is sound, you can seal the cracks with a flexible epoxy filler. This will give a tough but elastic surface which will adhere firmly to the timber, after which you can rub it down and re-paint. It is wise to put such fillers on to bare wood, for if they are put over paint, the only adhesion to the wood is via the paint film. If this loses its hold, obviously the filler must flake away.

Rot in the framework of a timber garage door will have to be cut away and new treated timber inserted. Do not try to fill gaps in the rotten wood with filler—it will not last.

If bolts work loose in timber doors, remove the bolts, drill out any soft wood, fill the holes with an epoxy filler and then when set, re-drill for new bolts. If you have difficulty undoing the rusted bolts, see chapter 4 which deals with metalwork, including the problems of rusting.

Timber doors may also sag with age because of their considerable size and weight. A metal bar used as a brace as shown in the illustration can pull the door back into place. Alternatively, you can use a straining wire as used for tensioning fencing; the screw-tightening device will allow you to tension the cable until it lifts the door the required amount. Obviously such jobs need the removal of the door and the door laying flat. As a further measure to remove the strain from a large door, fit a wheel castor so that the castor takes the weight when the door is open and closed. The illustration shows where to position this.

The up-and-over timber door can also present problems, very often because of bad design. On the same estate I referred to earlier, the timber up-and-over doors rotted away in the bottom panel because when the door was in the open position, the door panels were horizontal and the bottom one projected from the garage opening about 150 mm. If it were left open during rain, water dripped from the wall on to the panel, where it soon found its way into the timber, eventually causing rotting.

Again, such damage calls for the rotten wood to be cut away and new timber inserted. Then all cracks should be sealed with a mastic or flexible epoxy filler prior to re-painting.

Doors with natural finish

So far we have dealt with painted timber doors, but some of the trickier problems concern natural finishes where an attractive timber has been treated with a transparent coating so the wood grain shows through. By far the greatest problem is caused by the use of an unsuitable material in the past and the worst offender is linseed oil.

This looks attractive when first applied to bare hardwood, but given some months, it becomes sticky, attracts dust and loses its sheen. As far as I am concerned it is a material of the past, like whitewash, and it should not be used merely because it has been used previously.

It is best to use a chemical paint stripper, a scraper and fine wire wool to remove the old material down to bare wood, always working with the grain of the wood to avoid scratches. With the old oil off, rub down the wood with a fine grade glass-paper until the surface is really smooth—again be sure to work only with the wood grain. Scratches across the grain are practically impossible to lose and when you re-coat the timber, even the smallest scratches will show up.

Three ways of preventing a door sagging

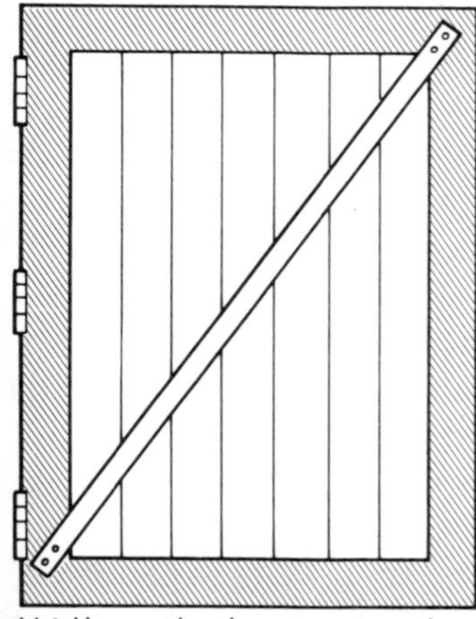

Metal bar as door brace on garage door

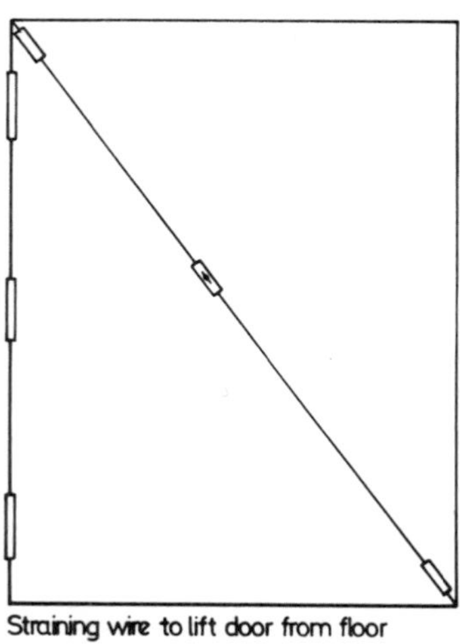

Straining wire to lift door from floor

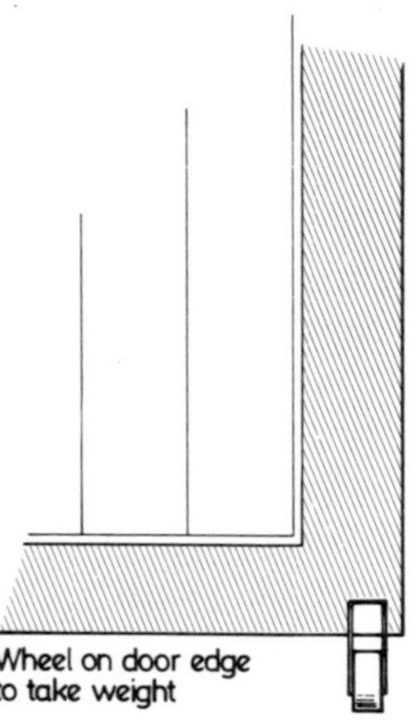

Wheel on door edge to take weight

If you want a glossy appearance to the door, there is still nothing to beat a good quality exterior varnish. The type of varnish supplied by a ship's chandler for use on boats is very durable. The first coat needs working well into the surface of the timber, then, when dry, it can be followed by two further coats.

An alternative is to use an exterior grade polyurethane varnish, but with this material, it is essential to ensure that no water can creep round the back of it and attack the finish from behind. Once it does this the varnish will peel.

Apart from glossy finishes, you have a choice of sheens. There are new preservative stain finishes in a number of attractive colours which soak into the wood giving complete protection against the weather, but without imparting a gloss. Then there are exterior grade teak oils for darker woods, siliconised to resist moisture penetration. These too impart a sheen rather than a gloss, and they allow the beauty of the wood grain to show through.

If you are planning to fit a new hardwood door, ask at the time of purchase what finish is recommended. Having installed the door, get the finish on as quickly as possible before dirt and grease get a hold.

Should you encounter cracks and gaps to fill during renovation, it will be necessary to use a stopping of the appropriate colour. Standard fillers would of course show up against the natural timber—even when coated with the new finish.

Unfortunately, timber is not a very stable material. It expands and contracts according to the moisture content, so that in winter a door may stick tight, while in the warm summer months it is an easy fit. The simplest way of dealing with this problem is to trim the door back on the sticking edge with a shaping tool or plane, then fit a flexible draught strip to seal the slight gap formed. The seal will take up the gap in summer and winter—with no more sticking. If the treatment has been applied to a front door exposed to the weather, it will also kill draughts.

Warping is another problem with older poor quality doors. This can be caused by facing one side of the door with hardboard or plywood so you get uneven expansion. You may solve the problem by facing the other side to act as a balancer. Failing that, you can try exerting pressure at one point. Note where the door closed first and put a wedge in at this point to stop the door closing all the way. Now force the door closed where it is not shutting properly, and keep it closed under pressure. This will help take the 'wind' out of the door.

Where a door is badly warped, it will pay you to discard it and fit a new one. Internal doors, which give most trouble, are still very reasonably priced.

Window frames

Timber frames give little trouble until the weather gets in. Then it is a question of steady deterioration as the paint is pushed off and more damp gets in. Very often an older frame will shrink away from the surrounding brickwork, forming a gap into which rain can be driven. Then the damp will attack from behind, with serious results.

Check for such gaps, and fill these with a mastic to keep the weather out. Never use putty or mortar as these set hard and if there should be any movement, they will crack away, letting in the damp once more. A mastic will stay flexible throughout its life; except on the surface, where it will harden off enough for you to be able to paint over it within a few days.

If sections of frame have become damp, wait until the timber dries out then examine it. If it hardens up, but just has fine cracks, fill these with a fine surface filler or exterior grade stopping before rubbing down and priming prior to painting. If the wood has become soft, so that you can dig a knife point in, you must cut back the damaged wood until you reach sound material, then insert a new piece. This can be glued in place using a waterproof resin adhesive, then fine gaps can be filled with fine surface filler or stopping.

Window frames tend to expand and contract with the moisture content, so these too may stick in the winter and work free in the summer. Very often a build-up of many coats of paint is the cause, and stripping back to the bare wood and starting the decoration again will solve the problem. If there is a sticking problem, use a shaping tool or plane to trim the frame, then fit flexible draught excluding strip to seal the resultant gap. This will make the window easy to operate, and it will ensure it is draught-proof during the winter months.

Where frames are in very poor condition, you can now buy special replacement frames in metal which are designed for the handyman. Or you can get standard joinery frames from a good timber merchant which will fit the cavities. Before choosing new frames consider very carefully whether they will be in character with the house. Modern picture window type frames may not suit your cottage style home.

Warped timber frames are a real problem, for it is not possible to apply any pressure to the frame without the risk of breaking the glass. You will have to take the frame out completely, remove the glass, then examine the twist. Damp the frame and apply a counter-twist, weighting the frame and holding it until it dries out. With a little experimentation you may get it back into shape—after which you can re-glaze and re-paint.

Never leave bare wood any longer than you can help. Get the priming coat on as quickly as possible, and keep the frame in the dry.

This is why it is wise to plan your decorating in manageable stages. Wood need never be left bare from one decorating session to another.

How to treat an oak sill prior to painting

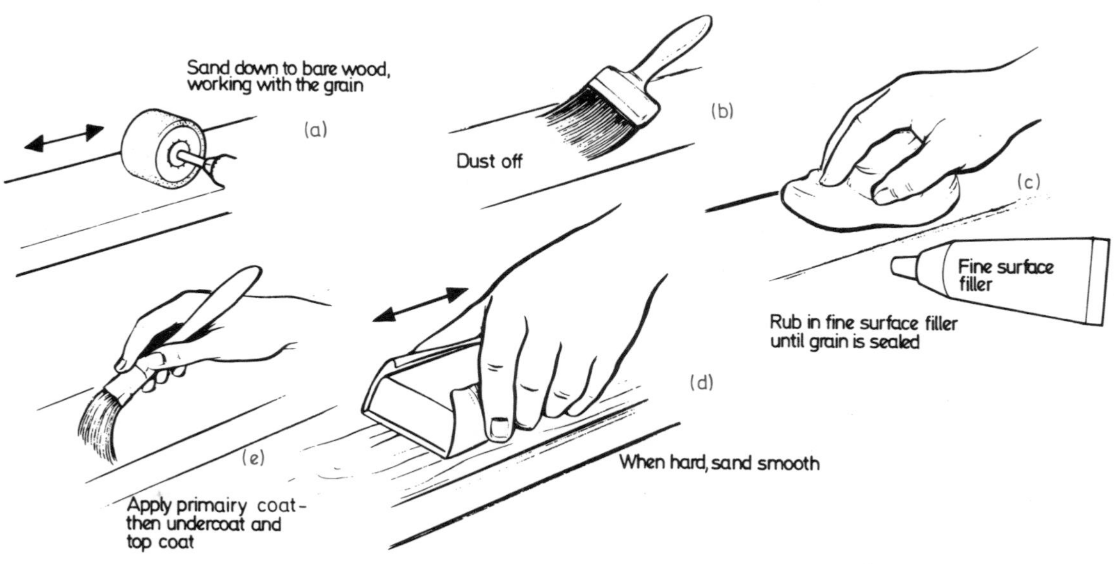

Window sills

Window sills often present a problem, because it is a surface over which water runs regularly during the winter months. Very often, part of the problem is that oak sills have been fitted to make them weather better—but oak and paint do not go well together! The reason for this is that air is trapped in the grain of the oak and when the sun shines on it, the air expands enough to push off the paint.

If you encounter oak, strip it down to bare wood, then work fine surface filler into the grain, pressing it in with a rag. Larger cracks can be sealed with an epoxy resin filler, then once set, it should be rubbed smooth and primed in the usual way.

Softwood sills are not so weather-resistant and, in this case, a damaged sill should be stripped to the bare wood. Check with a pointed knife for soft, rotten wood. If you find any, it must be cut out and new timber inserted. If sound, fill cracks with an epoxy filler or fine surface filler; rub smooth when hard, then prime as soon as possible. Do not neglect the end grain, for this is where the damp gets in fastest. Also examine the underside of the sill. There should be what is called a drip groove which encourages water to drip off rather than reach the wall surface.

Very often this groove becomes filled in with coats of paint. If this has occurred, strip off the paint to bare wood, gouge out the drip groove, then prime and re-paint.

If the sill has no groove, it will pay to pin a fine strip of hardwood beading to the underside of the sill before you paint. This will have the same effect as a groove. If you find gaps between the sill and the wall, fill them with a mastic. This is another point of entry for damp.

With your timberwork once more in good shape, it is vital to ensure that the weather cannot find a way in. Make sure that the putty in frames is sound and not cracking away. If pieces can be prised out, remove all loose material, brush out any dirt or dust, and apply a coat of priming paint before you re-putty (see chapter 8 for re-glazing tips). When you re-paint the putty (after allowing a week for the surface to harden) take the paint just on to the glass so you get a seal between putty and glass. Once the water finds an entry point here, you can get frames rotting from inside.

Main timbers

Where you encounter trouble with main structural timbers, such as floor joists, ceiling joists and rafters, you would be wise to seek professional guidance before cutting them out and replacing.

The borough surveyor, contacted through the town hall or municipal offices will advise you—and this may be an area where it will pay to sub-contract the work.

Floorboards

Many people who buy older properties encounter problems with the floors. These are subjected to considerable punishment, and as timber moves and shrinks with the years, you may have anything from irregular surfaces, to actual movement. Let us look at some of the problems you may meet.

Gaps

Some old floors had boards butted together, and as the boards have shrunk—particularly with the introduction of central heating—quite large gaps may appear.

If the floor is sound and well secured, large gaps can be filled by cutting a batten to a slight wedge shape, and tapping the batten into the gap after coating with adhesive (a pva adhesive would do). When the adhesive has set, plane down the strips as near the floor as you can, then finish off with a drum sander.

Smaller gaps can be filled with papier mâché. This is pressed into the cracks, working it well down; allowed to set hard, then rubbed smooth. It is a very old remedy, but still as effective as ever. Both battens and papier mâché can be stained if necessary to match surrounding boards. It is best to experiment, erring on the light side, as stains tend to dry darker than you expect.

If gaps appear in a poorly laid tongued and grooved floor, you have a bigger problem. It is not practicable to fill the gaps. The professional approach would be to lift the boards and re-lay them, tightening them up and filling the final gap with a new board. This is possible if you have the house empty and you have time to work on the house. If this is not possible you can cover the whole floor with hardboard, providing the floor is sound and well fixed. This will provide a good surface for floorcoverings of any kind.

You can fix the board with deep drive panel pins, or for insurance against the pins springing out, with small ring nails. Bear in mind that a board floor gives no access underneath. If you need to get at gas points or junction boxes, it will pay you to make removable panels, fixing them in place with small countersunk screws.

Wear

Where boards are slightly worn, forming hollows, hire a floor sanding machine and take the boards down to form a new surface. Do be sure to remove all old tacks and pins, and hammer down any proud floor nails, or you will ruin the belt on the sander.

Where boards are badly worn but still sound, if you have the opportunity to lift the boards you could turn them, to give you a brand new surface on the top. Obviously this is a long job, and it is not easy to lift the boards. The illustration overleaf shows you how this is done. Obstinate nails may have to be hammered down rather than drawn.

Removing and replacing damaged timber

Don't try to patch damaged wood

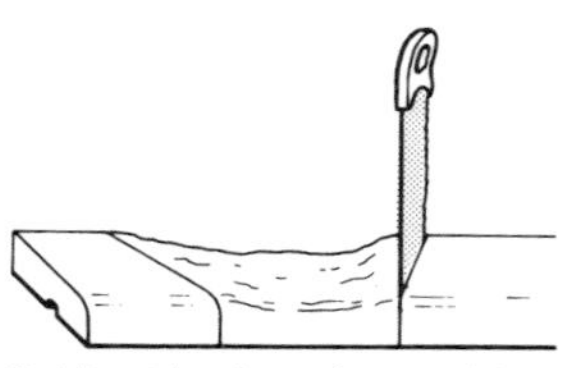
Cut it out, leaving only sound timber

Treat with preservative

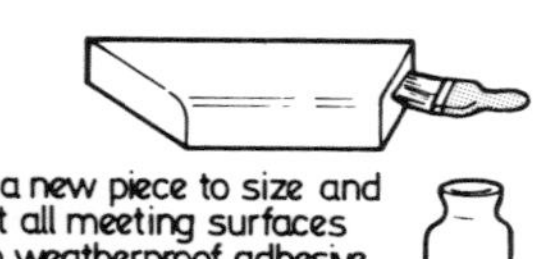
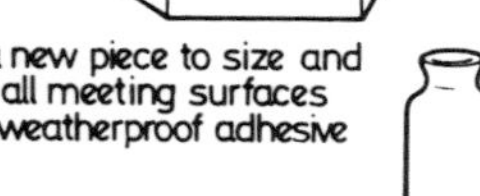
Cut a new piece to size and coat all meeting surfaces with weatherproof adhesive

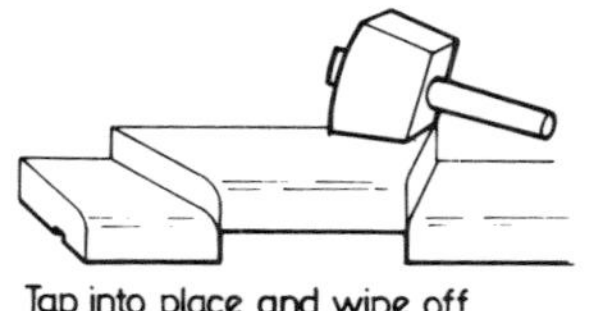
Tap into place and wipe off surplus adhesive

Sand smooth. Fill any gaps with fine surface filler

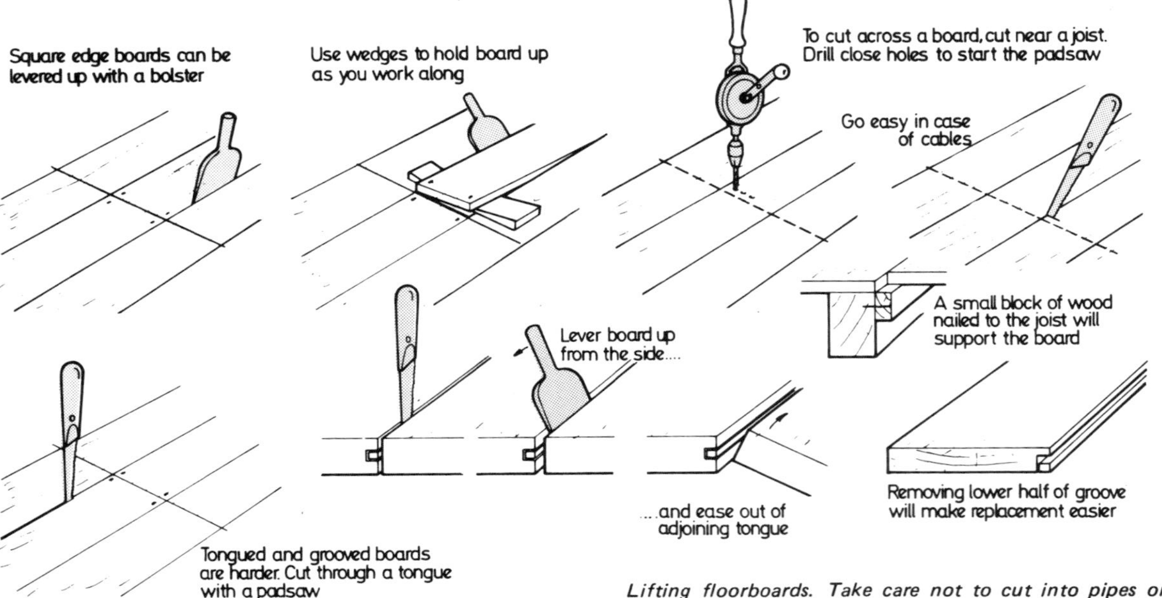

Lifting floorboards. Take care not to cut into pipes or cables

When dealing with an upper floor of an older house, hammering may be out of the question as it would bring the ceiling plaster down. This is another case for covering the floor with hardboard to give a new surface.

If floorboards are in bad shape, and springing badly, it will be necessary to form a tougher surface than hardboard. In this case, flooring grade chipboard could be laid over the old floor, screwing it in place with countersunk screws. This too presents problems, because it will raise floor levels. It may not affect the skirtings too much, but you may have to saw a strip off all the doors and you will need a chamfered beading to lose the little steps you will have formed.

Where the floor has to be removed because of serious rot, it will be simpler to lay flooring grade chipboard instead of floorboards. Far less fixing is necessary, and you will have a far smoother surface than you would get with floorboards, however carefully laid.

For fixing, drill clearance holes for screw heads at joist positions, countersink the holes with a rose countersink bit, then secure with countersunk head screws.

Movement

In an older house, you may find that the whole floor is moving on the joists. This is a more difficult problem to cure because it probably means that the joists are loose in the holes in which they rest, or the wall plates holding them have failed.

It will be necessary to gain access to the joist ends by lifting the floor, then you will have to re-anchor the joist ends by wedging them firm. If you find this job too difficult, you may be able to compromise by opening up the floor for a tradesman to get at the fault, allowing him to do the repair work, then leaving you to put the boards back. In this way you could considerably reduce labour charges.

Whenever you do expose joists or other supporting timber, it will pay you to treat the exposed timber with a preservative. Look upon it as an insurance policy against any future trouble.

Parquet flooring

If you inherit parquet or strip flooring, this may have been neglected over the years, leaving it looking very rough and scuffed. This is another situation where it will pay you to hire a floor sanding machine for a full day or weekend. The sander can be used to take off the top surface of the timber, exposing new wood, and it can look as new as the day it was first put down. Having got it clean and smooth, it is vital to get the wood sealed immediately before dirt and scuff marks can ruin it again.

Apply a polyurethane seal with a lint-free rag such as an old handkerchief wrapped around a ball of cotton wool. Work the sealer well into the wood and leave it to dry. When hard, give it a light rub with very fine glasspaper—not hard enough to scratch the wood surface. Then dust free and apply one or two more coats of seal, this time with a brush. If you want a glossy finish you can buy seal to give this. If you prefer it there is a seal which produces a matt sheen.

If the floor is in a reasonable condition which does not warrant sanding, but where scuff marks are spoiling the appearance, remove the marks and any accumulated dirt with fine wire wool dipped in turps substitute. Always rub with the wood grain—never across. This is to ensure you do not make scratches which cannot be removed. When the floor is clear of marks, give a light rub over with fine glasspaper, dust clean, then seal with one or two coats of polyurethane seal.

If you find loose blocks, prise them up, clean out all traces of accumulated dirt from underneath, and dig out any hard adhesive. Then use a bitumen-base adhesive or a black rubber adhesive to stick the blocks back. Try to keep adhesive off the face of the flooring blocks; such materials are not easy to remove. Where you find small gaps remaining, smooth down matching wood stopping to fill them. When set, smooth down with fine glasspaper, working only with the grain of the surrounding wood.

Skirting boards

The skirting board is designed to hide the joint between a wall and a floor, usually being fixed to the wall so the floor can move under it. Where a board has pulled away, you will find that it is nailed to plugs in the wall, and either the nails or the plugs have worked loose. Prise the board away, clean out all loose material from behind, plug the wall where necessary using a modern wall plug to match up with new countersunk holes in the board.

If you plan to add extra power socket outlets, this is the ideal time to run your new cable. It is not often you can gain access to the wall behind a skirting board.

Where you have the chance to re-site the boards it is a good idea to lift the board about 6–8 mm (½–¾ in) from the floor then re-fix it. This forms a gap into which carpet can be pushed when you are laying it, giving a very neat finish.

Where a skirting board has rotted, replace it with new treated timber. If you are working on an exterior wall where you feel damp may have struck through, treat the wall area with a damp repelling liquid of the type which soaks deep into the masonry. Then fix the new board with aluminium alloy countersunk screws.

Chapter 4 Metalwork

As timber is attacked by insect and rot, so iron and steel are under constant threat by rust and corrosion. All that is required is damp air in contact with bare metal, and it is just a matter of time before you have a heap of useless oxide of iron. Translate this problem into damaged window frames, rusting car bodywork, seized nuts and bolts and sagging gutters, and it represents destruction measured in hundreds of millions of pounds a year—to say nothing of the inconvenience caused.

The basic point to remember is that if you exclude air from the metal in some way, no rusting will take place. Therefore, dealing with the problem of rust falls into two main categories; prevention and elimination.

Protecting metal

Oils and greases

A fairly recent method of rust prevention is to use a fine protective oil in aerosol form. If the oil is sprayed on to all the exposed metal parts of, say, a lawnmover, it will form a fine, unbroken film which actually pushes water off and keeps the air away. It will evaporate after a while, so regular repeat coating is advisable. During the winter months, after a good spray, one coat should see you through to spring.

Oil spray applied to the undersides of mudguards and car wings will discourage a build-up of dirt. It will also ensure good electrical contact where wiring is exposed to the elements.

Metal garden and hand tools will benefit from a coating of oil, especially if stored out of doors. Keep an oily rag in a screw-top jam jar, and as you finish with tools like saws and chisels, given them a rub over with the rag before putting away. When you come to use them, it only takes a second to rub off the oil film with an old towel, and your tools will be in perfect condition.

Items like bolt threads, gate mechanisms and pulley wheels which are exposed to the elements need something heavier than fine oil, as this evaporates too quickly. A grease is more effective, but make sure that this does not come into contact with hands or clothes. Keep a pot of grease handy and an old paintbrush to spread it. Always make a regular check on metalwork that needs protecting.

Chemical protection

Special papers which are chemically impregnated are available; the idea being that fumes are given off which prevent metal rusting. Obviously the chemical is most effective in a confined space, so you can use it in drawers, boxes, and glass containers housing metal objects. If a strip of this paper is kept with screws and nails in a screw-top jar, they will stay bright. If you wish to store spare ironmongery in plastic bags, slip a piece of peper in each bag before sealing.

While on the subject of storing, never store metal items in jars or plastic bags without some protection. You could be sealing moist air in the bag, which could cause more rusting than if they had been left in the fresh air.

An alternative to the paper is silica gel crystals. These crystals have the ability to absorb considerable quantities of water, so if placed in a container they will keep

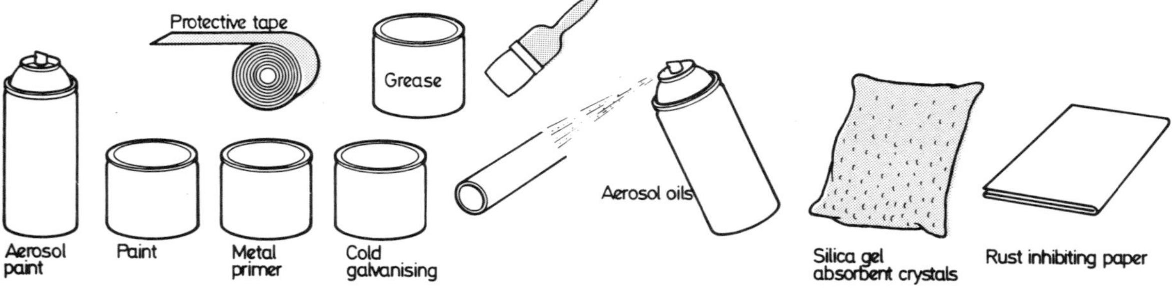

Ways of treating metal to prevent rust and corrosion

the air inside dry—until the crystals are saturated. Once this point is reached, you merely place the crystals in the oven and dry out the water. The crystals are then ready for use again. You can buy tell-tale crystals which change colour as they become overloaded with water. This can be useful, especially during a winter storage period when the items are not in use.

Do not wrap tools in old rags or newspapers to protect them; both these absorb moisture from the air until quite damp, and you will be merely holding the damp in contact with the metal. Rag is suitable as long as it is well soaked in a protective oil.

Tapes

Although used mainly in industry, special tapes are available for covering metal or for winding round pipes, where they are to be perhaps buried in the ground. Again, the simple principle applies. The tape keeps air and moisture away from the metal, so there is no corrosion.

Paints

There is nothing new about rust-resisting paint, and it should be used where items are to be handled, making oils and greases impractical. The metal must be clean and grease-free, then it should be painted with a metal primer, followed by a good quality exterior grade paint. For durability choose a polyurethane paint. Ensure that all of the metal is treated. Gaps in the system can allow localised rusting which can soon spread. If you accidentally scratch or chip the paint coating, deal with it as soon as possible before the surface rusts.

A cold galvanising paint gives excellent protection to a metal surface. This is a zinc-rich paint with the zinc held in a binding agent. Stir the paint well to mix the two together before applying to a clean, dry surface. The zinc coating will resist rusting, and once it has set, it can be painted in the normal way.

Alternatives to metal

A different approach to prevention is to consider what alternatives there are to metal when constructing or repairing. There are many materials now available which will not corrode or rust; if you can choose from these you have a distinct advantage.

Nails and screws are available in aluminium alloy and some are galvanised. Hinges are available in nylon; gutters, downpipes and waste systems made in pvc are quite common; and even chromium plating can be imitated in acrylic plastics. It is obviously sensible to choose materials which do not corrode and which need little or no maintenance.

Dealing with rust

Where you encounter rust, all loose material must be removed down to sound metal. For this you can use a hand-held wire brush, or a wheel or cup brush mounted in a power tool. Whichever you choose, be sure to wear protective goggles as you can suffer eye damage from the flying particles. Special toughened plastic safety glasses are not expensive, and they will allow you to work in complete safety.

If dealing with a rusted metal window frame, be sure you get to the source of the rust, even if you have to strip off a lot of extra paint. It is no use at all painting over rust, as the action will continue under the paint and eventually push your new coating off.

When you are back to sound metal, rub over with fine emery paper to smooth the metal, then dust off and apply a cold galvanising paint or a chemical rust inhibitor. This is a special liquid which either converts the iron oxide to iron phosphate, or forms an inert tannate film. Read the instructions carefully before you use it, both to see how it is applied, and also whether it needs neutralising after use. Once the rust killer has done its work, you can apply a metal primer, followed by the normal paint coating.

When using these chemicals, be sure to protect your eyes against splashing. The safety glasses will protect you.

In severe cases, you may find the metal eaten away to form a hollow—or at the worst a hole right through. It is best to be ruthless and file away all loose and flaking metal until you are back to solid material, rub clean and dust off. Then mix an epoxy resin filler—as much as you can use in about ten minutes (five in hot weather) and fill in the cavity proud of the surface. If there is a smallish hole, cover the far side with a piece of wood or hardboard covered in polythene. The polythene will ensure that the filler lets go when set.

When hard, you can rub back the filler until it is flush with the surrounding metal. Apply rust inhibitor to the surrounding metal, then prime and paint.

How to remove rust—and how to protect the clean metal

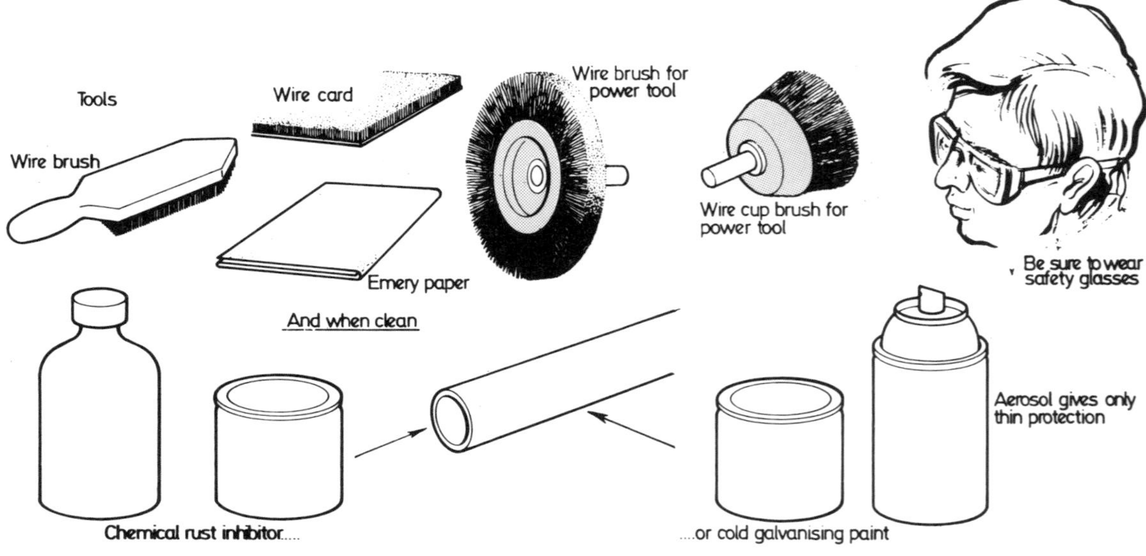

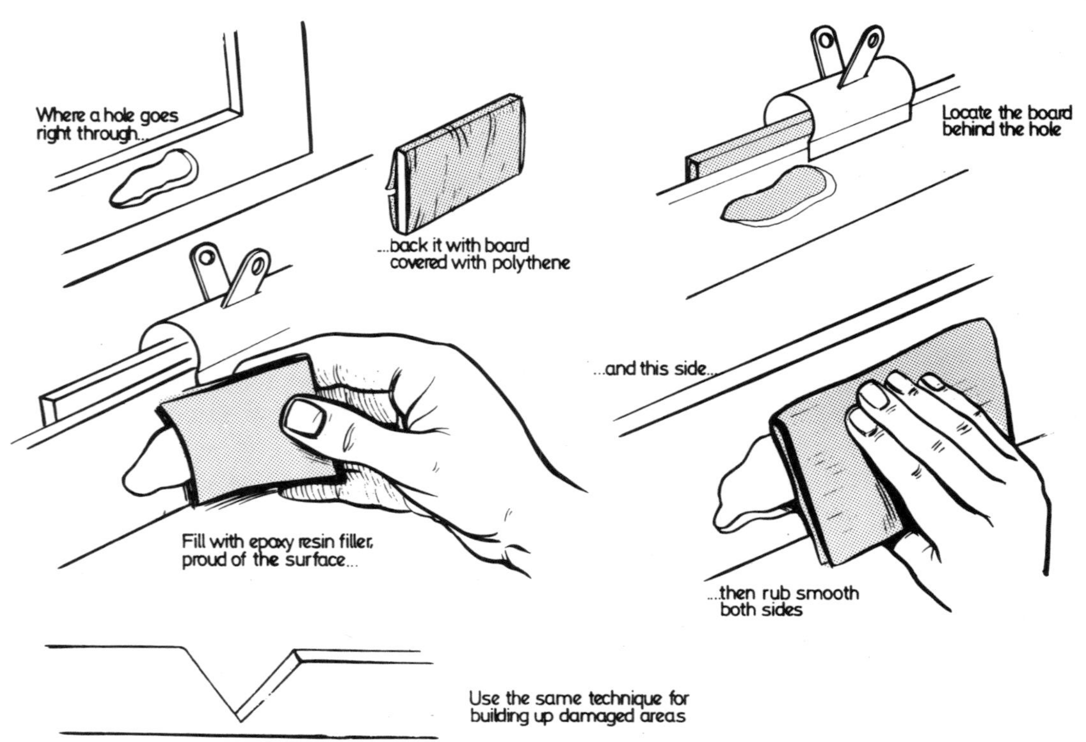

Filling holes in metalwork

Where you encounter a large hole, the filler will need support. You can give this by backing the hole with perforated metal sheeting sold for this purpose. Anchor the sheet in place with a little epoxy filler, then fill the hole as previously described. Allow to set, and rub smooth.

The epoxy filler can be used to build up damaged areas, such as where a cast iron gutter has a piece broken away. The area to be repaired must be clean and dry so that the filler can get a good grip, then you mould the filler to the required shape and let it set. Once hard it can be filed, drilled and sanded as for metal.

Where metal is badly rusted and no longer has any strength, it will be necessary to remove the damaged section completely and insert new metal. This job has been greatly simplified by the introduction of d-i-y welding equipment.

It pays to keep a selection of pieces of metal in your repair kit; these should be of various gauges (thicknesses) and types. A typical selection might be tinplate cut from old cans, thin sheet steel, brass and alloy. You can cut the thin material with tinsnips or with the pliers-type nibbling tool which has changeable cutting blades. Thicker materials need a hacksaw and a selection of small files for cleaning up.

If you intend to do much metalwork it will be necessary to add a heavy metal-working vice to your tool kit so that you have a firm and heavy surface in which to grip and work your metal. You will also need a set of high speed steel twist drills for drilling holes, and it will help considerably if you invest in a vertical drill stand. You will get much more accurate holes with less fear of breaking your drills.

When drilling metal, never hold the material in your fingers. If the twist drill snags up, it will rotate the metal violently, and you can get a very nasty cut. Treat all metal sheet with respect; it can be very sharp, and it would be wise to wear your leather gardening gloves if you are not used to metalworking.

Dismantling metalwork

One of the greatest time wasters in repair work is trying to dismantle rusted or corroded components. If you cannot separate the components you have little chance of repairing. If the trouble is minor, applying easing oil to the area to be stripped, or, if possible and you are sure no harm will be done, submerse the components in de-rusting fluid. Eventually the corrosion will dissolve and you will be able to apply a spanner or screwdriver.

However, there are situations where it is not possible to apply this technique, such as where the bolts holding the sections of a shed have rusted badly, but the nut and bolt are tight against the wood. Very often the bolt head has no slot, relying on a square on the shank to stop it turning. So if you force the nut, the whole unit revolves in the wood.

Where corrosion is not too severe, apply easing oil to the bolt thread where visible, then use a small hacksaw and file a slot in the bolt head. This will allow you to hold a screwdriver in the slot while you try to turn the nut. Hold the driver still by gripping its blade in a grip wrench.

If this fails, you can drill down into the bolt head, using a twist drill as near the size of the bolt shank as possible. It is a slow job, but eventually the head of the bolt will drop away and you will be able to withdraw the whole thing from the wood. Yet another alternative is to use a special nut splitting tool. This is applied to one flat of the nut and, as the splitter is tightened, it forces a sharp wedge into the metal, which it eventually splits, releasing the nut from the thread. Using this latter method, you can use the bolt again, merely finding a nut to fit it.

Before reassembling nuts and bolts, treat the thread with a special oil available which makes any future dismantling easy. Alternatively, you can use grease or Vaseline. Never use soap as this can encourage rusting and it certainly does not work as well as oil or grease.

On more delicate work where you do not wish to saw or drill, try applying the hot tip of a soldering iron to the bolt end.

Tips to make metalworking easier and safer

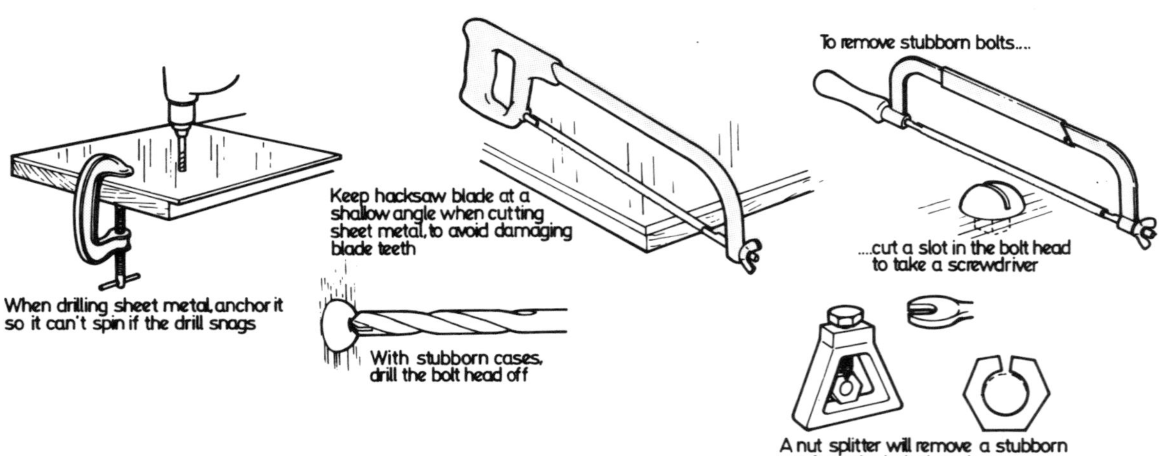

The heat will expand the metal, very often breaking the grip of the rust. When applying the spanner, force the nut just a shade tighter before trying to loosen. A trick which often succeeds where all else fails!

In some cases you may not want a nut to be loose, or it may vibrate loose when the equipment to which it is fixed vibrates. Where a nut must be secure, you can apply a second nut as a lock nut, or you can buy special nuts with a plastic insert which acts as a damper and a lock. You can also buy a special compound which, when applied to the thread, will ensure the nut does not work loose. This will not stop you undoing it with a spanner at some future date.

Chapter 5 Walls and ceilings

It is not so easy to write about walls nowadays, for building methods have changed quite considerably in recent years. At one time houses had solid walls or cavity walls mainly of brick, then lightweight blocks were introduced mainly for use on the interior wall. Today we have an increasing use of timber frame construction where only a decorative skin of brick is applied to the exterior after the main construction is complete.

Before you take on the job of wall repair or maintenance it will pay you to find out how your walls are constructed. Is the outer wall, for example, a structural part of the house? Is the stone or brick facing mainly decorative?

Settlement cracks

Settlement or movement can be a problem, and this is quite common, especially when we have long, dry summers. Soil can shrink and expand according to its water content, and this is most noticeable with clay soils. Unfortunately, if a house is standing on soil which moves, something has to give. This may only be the joints in a room between walls and ceiling; it may be a long but not very wide crack running across a large wall surface such as that on the stair well, or it may be the joint between a garage and the house wall to which it is attached.

Such seasonal movement is very difficult to hide. Indoors it can take the form of a cove cornice which can move the crack, and outside it may be a flashing which can move enough to disguise the crack. On inside decorated walls hiding the crack is not so easy. Most cellulose fillers used to fill cracks when they are open cannot withstand the tremendous pressure exerted when the crack closes during the winter months. They merely get crushed out so the gap is back next year. If the wall plaster is hard and strong, an epoxy type filler stands a better chance of survival, but you may merely get a new crack nearby.

Hessian type wallcoverings, grasscloth and similar materials disguise cracks by moving with them and, of course, sheet or strip wall panelling will also be effective. Anaglyptas are not normally successful as they have little shear strength.

Seasonal movement is nothing to worry about, apart from appearance, but what is far more serious is subsidence. This is

Settlement cracks—very common in dry weather

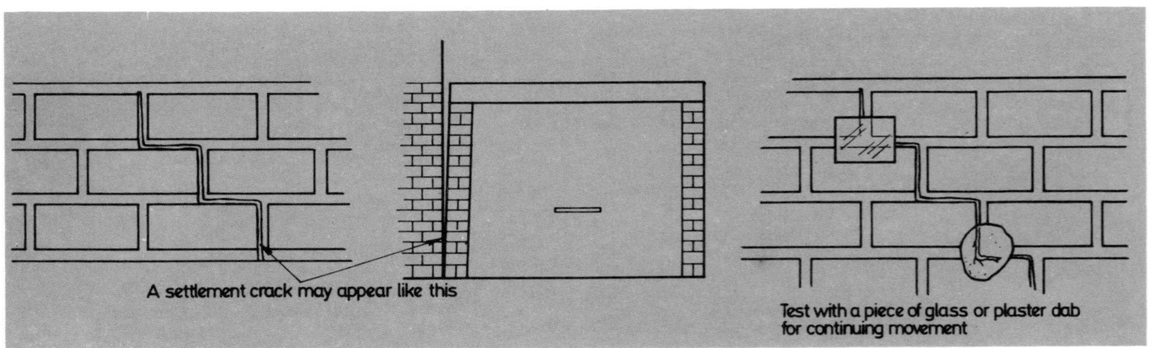

where the ground actually sinks, and it may be caused by building on land which has not settled sufficiently, for example putting new estates on covered rubbish tips. Worse still, the subsidence may be the after-effects of old mine workings where vibration or flooding has caused ground to collapse.

If you discover cracks which seem to continue widening rather than opening and shutting with the seasons, test the area by securing a piece of glass across the crack with epoxy resin adhesive. Make sure the adhesive gets a good grip on the brick. Alternatively, build up a flat blob of plaster of paris across the gap at a couple of points. Now wait to see what happens; as the structure moves, the glass will crack or the plaster break,and you will get a very clear picture of how much movement is involved.

Settlement is not the kind of problem you can deal with on your own, and if you suspect this trouble, call in to see your local borough surveyor and discuss the matter. He will know the area and the condition of the land upon which your home is built. If there is a serious settlement, then it may be necessary to have the foundations strengthened by underpinning. This can be an expensive process as considerable digging is involved down to and below foundation level.

Dealing with cracked mortar and damaged brickwork

If your house is fairly new, slight settlement cracks are quite commonplace. You will find that these usually follow the mortar joints and do not continue to expand. In such cases, all you need do is rake out any loose mortar, and fill with a new mortar mix. Damp the existing work first to cut suction, and be sure to use a very dry mix for filling so that you do not mark the surrounding brickwork. For smaller jobs, mortar supplied as a dry mix in paper sacks is the most economical. Merely add the minimum of water as required.

In older properties, you may find that the mortar pointing is crumbling. This needs replacing, so rake out the old mortar to a depth of about 12 mm (½ in). (The drawing overleaf shows a tool which can be made from a piece of scrap metal to do this job.) Then brush out the joints to remove dust, damp the gaps with water, then apply a dryish mix of mortar. The trickiest part of the job is getting a good finish to the joints. There are three basic finishes as illustrated, the hollow joint being the simplest.

Soft bricks which have become porous are often affected by the frost, causing flaking of the surface. Use a steel chisel and club hammer to cut into the brick about 25 mm (1 in), then you need to find a matching brick. Split this with a club hammer and bolster to give you a piece which can be inset over the damaged area, sticking it in place with mortar. Then re-point as for the rest of the wall. Having restored the area, apply a liberal coating of silicone water repellent to the bricks and pointing. This will ensure that the frost will not cause damage in future.

Cleaning brickwork

Where brickwork has become dirty, scrub it with a stiff brush and plenty of water. Do not use detergent or soap or you will get a whitish staining of the bricks which is impossible to lose.

A textured brick can often be improved by wire brushing, but be sure to protect your eyes. Another 'wrinkle' is to find a piece of matching brick, break it, and use a piece as a pumice block, scrubbing the

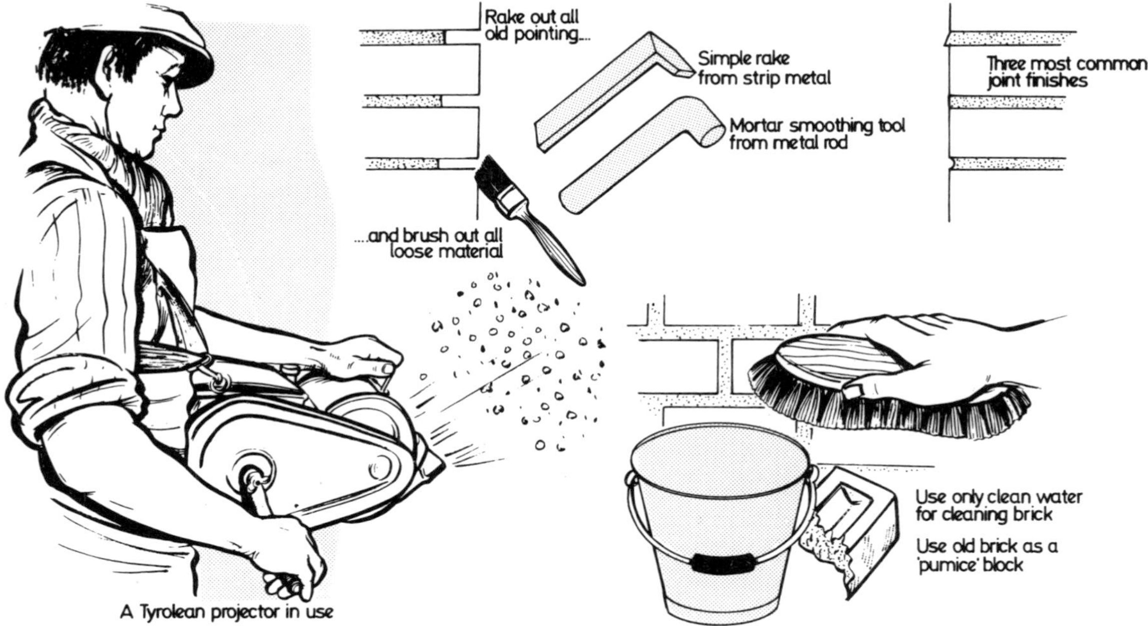

Ways of dealing with jaded walls

brickwork with it. This will rub away the grime without affecting the colouring of the brick in any way.

Very often grubby mortar can make a wall look dull. You can improve the appearance by raking back the mortar by about 8 mm (¾ in) and re-pointing with a lighter coloured mortar. You can order white cement for special jobs like this, which will lighten the mix. Again, keep the mix as dry as possible, so it does not mark the bricks, and damp the brickwork before adding the new material.

Wherever possible, avoid painting brickwork. It never looks good and once painted there is no way of getting the paint out of the pores of the brickwork. If the wall really looks dull, it is better to consider adding a new surface. The simplest method is to use what is called a Tyrolean projector. This is a special tool which can be used to fling a thin mortar mix on to the wall to produce an interesting textured surface. This tool can be borrowed from most hire shops, together with full details on how to make suitable mixes.

The advantage of this system is that it fills all the brick joints, giving a smooth but textured surface. This can then be painted with any of the exterior paints, from emulsion to stone paint.

Repairing rendered surfaces

Rendered wall surfaces can be painted with masonry paint. Do not worry about hair line cracks as a full bodied masonry paint will lose these. Large cracks should be cleaned and sealed with mortar. If some pva adhesive is added to the mixing water this will ensure good adhesion; then, when dry, you can paint.

Where rendered surfaces have been stained by mould growth, buy a special primer sealer to sterilise the wall and to prepare it for the new paint. With some cement-based paints you will be advised to use a sealer anyway, so be sure to check just what you need when buying your materials.

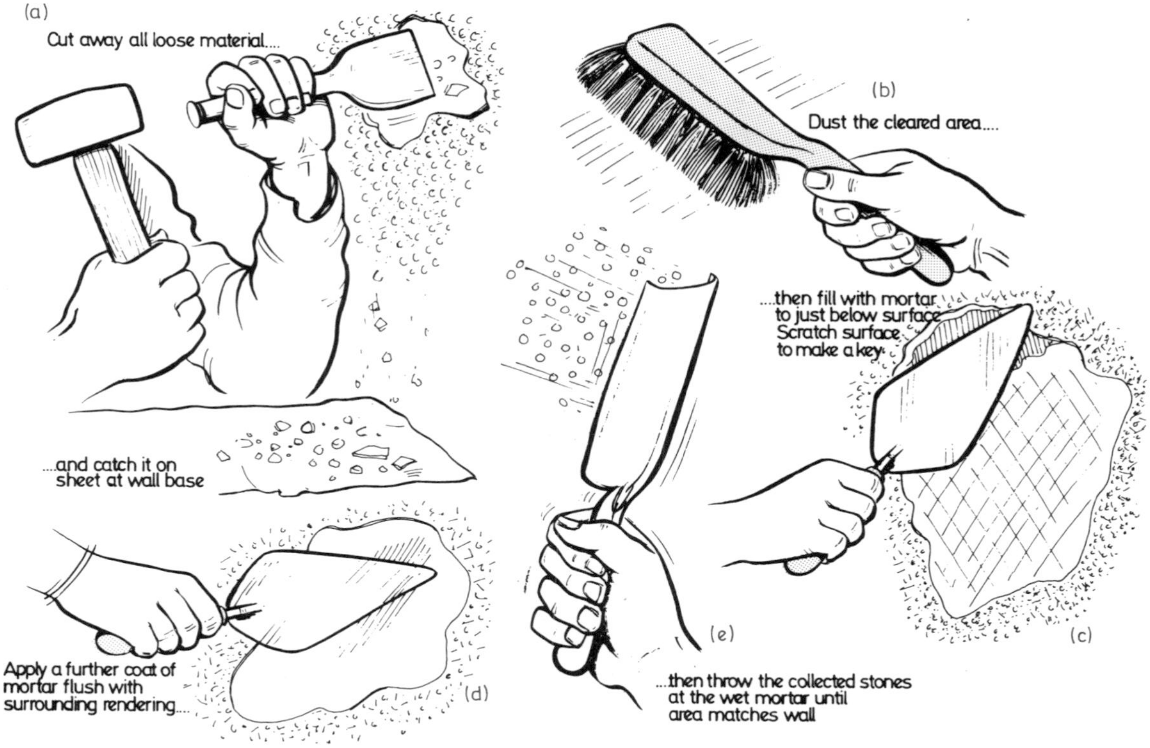

(a)
Cut away all loose material....
...and catch it on sheet at wall base
(b)
Dust the cleared area....
....then fill with mortar to just below surface Scratch surface to make a key
(c)
Apply a further coat of mortar flush with surrounding rendering....
(d)
(e)
...then throw the collected stones at the wet mortar until area matches wall

How to repair damaged pebbledash

(a)
Dig out all loose material
Dust well, then damp with water
(b)
(c)
Apply filler with flexible scraper blade. Leave proud of surface
(e)
(d)
On large areas, use a steel straight-edge to scrape filler smooth
When set, smooth down with sanding block

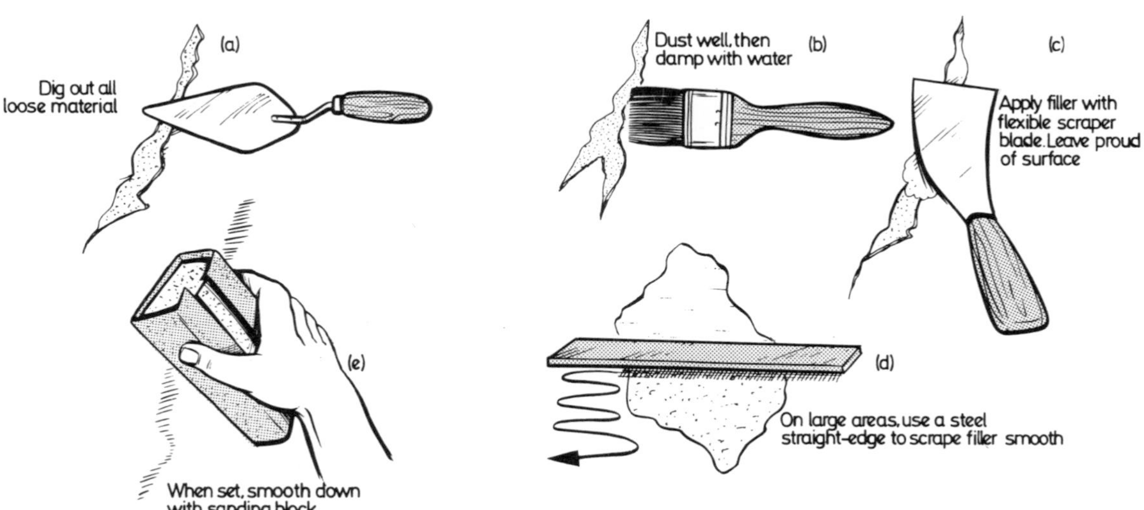

Repairing damaged wall rendering

Pebbledash and spar dash can be painted, and the best tool to use is the shaggy hair exterior grade nylon paint roller. If you prefer a brush, use one at least 127 mm (5 in) wide, or use a sweeping brush of the type you use with a dustpan. You will find the handle of this type of brush very comfortable to use.

Unfortunately, the layer of mortar holding the stones can bulge away from the wall with age, and this is far too unstable a surface to redecorate. Spread sacking or sheet polythene along the wall, then hack off the damaged areas using a bolster and club hammer, protecting your eyes. When the damaged areas are clear, sort out the rubbish and rescue all the old stones, place these in water to clean and wet them. This is a better idea than buying new stones, as new ones will be far brighter and cleaner, and the repair will be very noticeable.

Brush clean the bare areas, damp with water, then add a layer of cement mortar. If the repair is shallow, only one application is necessary. If the holes are deep, apply one layer to within 6 mm (¼ in) of the surface, allow it to start to harden, say half an hour, then scratch the surface with a trowel point to form a key for the next coat. With the top coat in place, throw the stones on to the wet mortar, pressing them lightly with a piece of board to ensure they are anchored and that they match the surrounding area.

Where the dash is in a really bad state, it will be necessary to pull the lot off, in which case the simplest way of redecorating is to use the Tyrolean projector already described.

Treatment of outside timbers

If your home is part-faced with timber, this should be treated as for the rest of the paintwork if already painted. If treated with a natural finish, give it a liberal coat of matching wood preservative. If you have red cedar timbering, there is a special grade of preservative; which includes stain, designed to re-colour the cedar to its approximate original colouring. Cedar shingles should be treated in a similar way, and it is wise to give them a regular coating so the wood does not dry right out and curl. Be sure to fix loose timberwork with alloy or galvanised nails so you do not get staining.

Plastic boarding is quite common, and this should need no treatment other than a good wash down with water and detergent to remove grime. Do not use abrasives as you will merely roughen the surface and encourage dirt to stick. Do not use chemical solvents as these will soften and mark the plastic. Of course never, ever, use a blow-torch!

Repairing interior plaster walls

Interior walls where the plaster is in good condition usually need little treatment. You may encounter minor cracks, plus holes where fitments have been put up in the past. These should be cleaned of loose material, damped with water and filled with cellulose filler. Always fill just proud of the surface, then rub back with glass-paper until level with the surrounding wall.

Where pieces of plaster have dropped out, tap the wall and listen for a hollow sound. If it does sound hollow, you will need to cut back the plaster until you reach solid material. Dust clean, then damp and apply some filler such as Keene's cement to within 5 mm (¼ in) of the surface. Allow the filler to start to set, then scratch the surface to give a key for new material, then apply a top coat, smoothing it just proud of the surface. When hard, use glasspaper to get a really smooth surface.

In some older properties you may find the plaster is in very poor shape, perhaps pulling away with the old wallpaper. In this case there is no point in patching. The whole lot needs to be hacked off to the brickwork—this is a really messy job! There will be a lot of dust, and to keep it down it is a good idea to damp the plaster thoroughly before hacking it away. Replastering is not a job for the inexperienced, and it will pay you to get a plasterer to resurface the wall. The alternative is to dry line the wall, using sheet plasterboard—and this you can do yourself.

Lining walls

The standard way of lining used to be to fix timber battens to the wall to which the plasterboard could be nailed. With the introduction of new adhesive plasters, it is now possible to apply blobs of special plaster to the cleaned wall, then press the sheet plasterboard in place. Jointing is the most difficult of the fixing operations, and this is done with a special jointing tape and finishing plaster, full details of which can be obtained when buying the boards.

An advantage of dry lining is, as the name implies, that there is no water to dry out after the job is done, as there is with wet plastering. So, once joints are dry, you can start redecorating.

If you plan to do any rewiring, such as fixing wall lights, remember the ideal time to do it is before putting on the sheet plasterboard. You can channel the wall to recess the cables to the lights, then lose the lot under the board. You will, of course, need holes in the plasterboard large enough to feed the cable through.

You may also have to remove skirting boards before lining, and then replace them over the top of your new wall surface. This is the ideal time for the fixing of new socket outlets as you can arrange the wiring behind the plasterboard, then merely fix your new sockets when the new wall is finished.

Filling gaps between walls and ceiling

We have already considered slight movement of the house on its foundations, and a weak spot for cracking is the joint between the walls of a room and the ceiling. Filling at this point has little effect, so the best solution is to fit a coving to bridge the gap. The simplest type is made of expanded polystyrene, but this has problems in that it comes in short lengths which have to be butt jointed. Losing the joints is very difficult as polystyrene is hard to smooth. It tends to rough up as you rub it.

The best coving is made of gypsum plaster. This is far heavier to handle, but very attractive when fixed. Again, the introduction of adhesive plasters makes it possible to stick it in place with no other support necessary. It can be obtained in long lengths if you wish to have the minimum of joints; shorter lengths are available if you find them easier to handle. Cutting is simple enough, but making the mitres for internal and external corners calls for a little practice. You can get some very odd shapes, even though a template is supplied.

Ceiling faults

This brings us to the ceiling, and here it is the older property which will give us most trouble. The old system of making a ceiling was to fix laths to the ceiling joists with a small gap between each lath. Then a special fibrous plaster was pressed on the laths so that is squeezed up between them and keyed itself in. Then a finishing coat was applied. Old age, plus severe vibration over the years may have broken the keying and, in consequence, you can get sagging in places.

Where the damage is slight, it is possible to use alloy screws to screw the plaster back to the laths. Or, if you can gain access to the underfloor above, such as in the loft, you can press the ceiling back into place with a length of timber and piece of board. Then pour a fairly wet mix of Keene's cement, or even plaster of Paris over the damaged section to form a new key.

Where the ceiling is in a bad way, it will have to come down, and this is an extremely messy job, because of the dust. As with stripping walls, it is wise to damp down the ceiling plaster to reduce the dust while you pull it and the laths away from the ceiling. You can then replace the laths with ceiling plasterboard, nailed with special plasterboard nails to the joints. The joints will have to be sealed with a special jointing tape and finishing plaster.

If you want a simpler solution, leave the joints and cover the whole ceiling with one of the plastic compounds designed for texturing. By the time it is stippled or combed you will not see the joists and you will have hidden the nails.

The modern plasterboard ceiling does not present such drastic problems. The most common one is slight cracking at the joints. This is often caused in bedrooms by loading too much in the loft and these cracks are not easy to lose. A lining paper often helps, or you can use one of the plastic compounds already referred to.

Where a ceiling looks in poor condition through cracking, but is holding up well, the simplest disguise is to use one of the many designs of expanded polystyrene or fibreboard ceiling tiles. If you choose expanded polystyrene, remember you must apply adhesive over the whole ceiling area, ***not in blobs.*** This is to ensure that, should there be a fire, no burning pieces of expanded polystyrene will drop away. If you prefer something with more fire resistance, there are fibreboard and textured plasterboard tiles. They are more expensive, and considerably heavier than plastic tiles, but are still well within the scope of the d-i-y enthusiast.

Ceiling types—and how to apply expanded polystyrene tiles

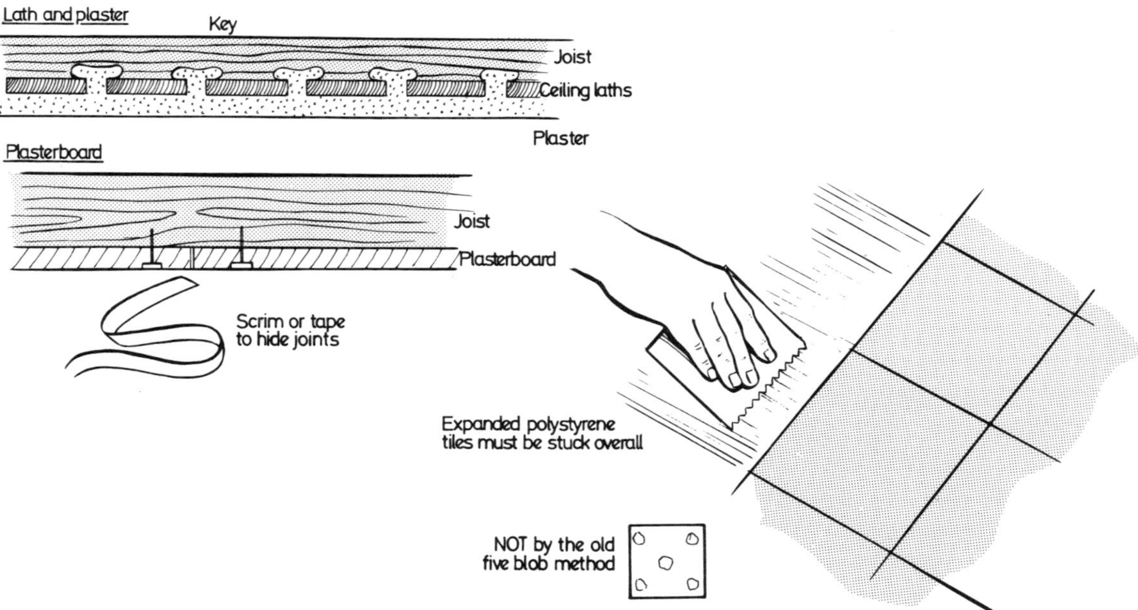

Stains may also be a nuisance. The cause may be a burst pipe or leaking tank some time in the past which carried rust into the ceiling which may bleed through your paint. It may also have been caused by an over-zealous operator applying older type wood-worm killers and letting the fluid seep through the ceiling. Before decorating, and assuming the stains are dry, apply a liberal coat of aluminium primer sealer to the stained area. This has a scale-like construction which effectively seals off the stain and, once dry, you can decorate over it. Do not confuse this material with aluminium paint which has not the same qualities. The aluminium in the latter is finely ground and does not have the same sealing properties.

Failure of new decorations to stick firmly to the ceiling can be most annoying, and the most common reason for this is that in the past distemper was used for decoration. This has a chalky quality, and nothing will adhere to it. The only treatment is to remove it by rubbing with a coarse rag and plenty of water until you get down to bare plaster. Thick areas can be damaged then scraped off, holding a dustpan underneath to catch the mess. Hard deposits can be sealed with a special distemper sealer.

Mould growth

Both walls and ceilings which become damp can encourage the growth of mould spores. These are harmless, but they do ruin decoration, staining areas with brownish spots.

Such trouble must be dealt with by removing the wall covering and treating the bare plaster with a fungicide. This will kill off the spores. As an extra precaution, use a paste containing a fungicide when re-papering.

Chapter 6
Damp

Damp, in all its forms, does very serious damage to most building materials; it will rot timbers, rust metal and ruin all forms of decoration. Damp should be treated very seriously, and for this reason, we have a chapter solely devoted to it, even though it is mentioned in other chapters. Wherever damp is encountered, the rule is to deal with it as soon as possible, for the longer it is left, the more serious will be the problems of repair. This, in turn, means more expense.

There are three main sources of damp; rain penetration, moisture rising from the soil, and moisture-laden air which leads to condensation. All three are considered in this chapter.

The roof

This is the area which receives the brunt of any rainfall, so it must be in good condition. Unfortunately it is the most difficult area to check and to repair. You should make it a rule that no roof work is attempted without the correct means of access. This means a ladder extending at least three rungs above gutter height; then a correct roof ladder which is designed to hook firmly over the roof ridge. This combination will ensure that you have a safe means of getting to the roof, and something firm to hang on while you work. Make sure you erect the ladder at the correct angle—1 metre out for every 4 metres up (or 3 ft for every 12 ft). Also make sure that the base of the ladder is anchored so it cannot slip.

Examine the ridge tiles. They should all be firmly anchored in place, but frost may have attacked the mortar and broken the bond. If you have deeply profiled tiles, you may find that gaps are also filled with mortar; this is termed pargeting. This mortar too may work loose, or you may find that if it is on the soft side the birds will peck it out to gain access to the loft for nesting. Any mortar in this condition should be replaced.

Damaged or displaced tiles need replacing or putting back. If you live in an older house with a slate roof, check that the nails are still in good condition. A common fault is that the nails corrode away, allowing the slates to slide. It is wise to remove any moss growth as you proceed. Remove the moss with a small trowel, then brush with moss killer.

Now move over to the chimney stack and see that the general condition of the brickwork is good. In older properties where there has been damp in the flue lining, and perhaps deposits of corrosive chemicals from fuel burned, you may find the mortar has been badly damaged, and it could be that the stack is unsafe. This is a job where you should get professional advice, for the sheer weight of this brickwork makes it quite unmanageable unless you have roof scaffolding and the correct equipment.

If the stack is sound, check the mortar holding any chimney pots. This is called the flaunching and any damage needs putting right. If the fireplaces below are no longer in use, cover the unused pots with a half round tile, fixing each in place with cement mortar. This will prevent rain getting down the flue and perhaps causing damp patches on bedroom walls.

In an older property where this is a stack for a boiler, check to see that the flue has a liner between the boiler and the chimney pot. When inefficient stoves were used in the past a lot of heat went up the flue. This did not matter too much

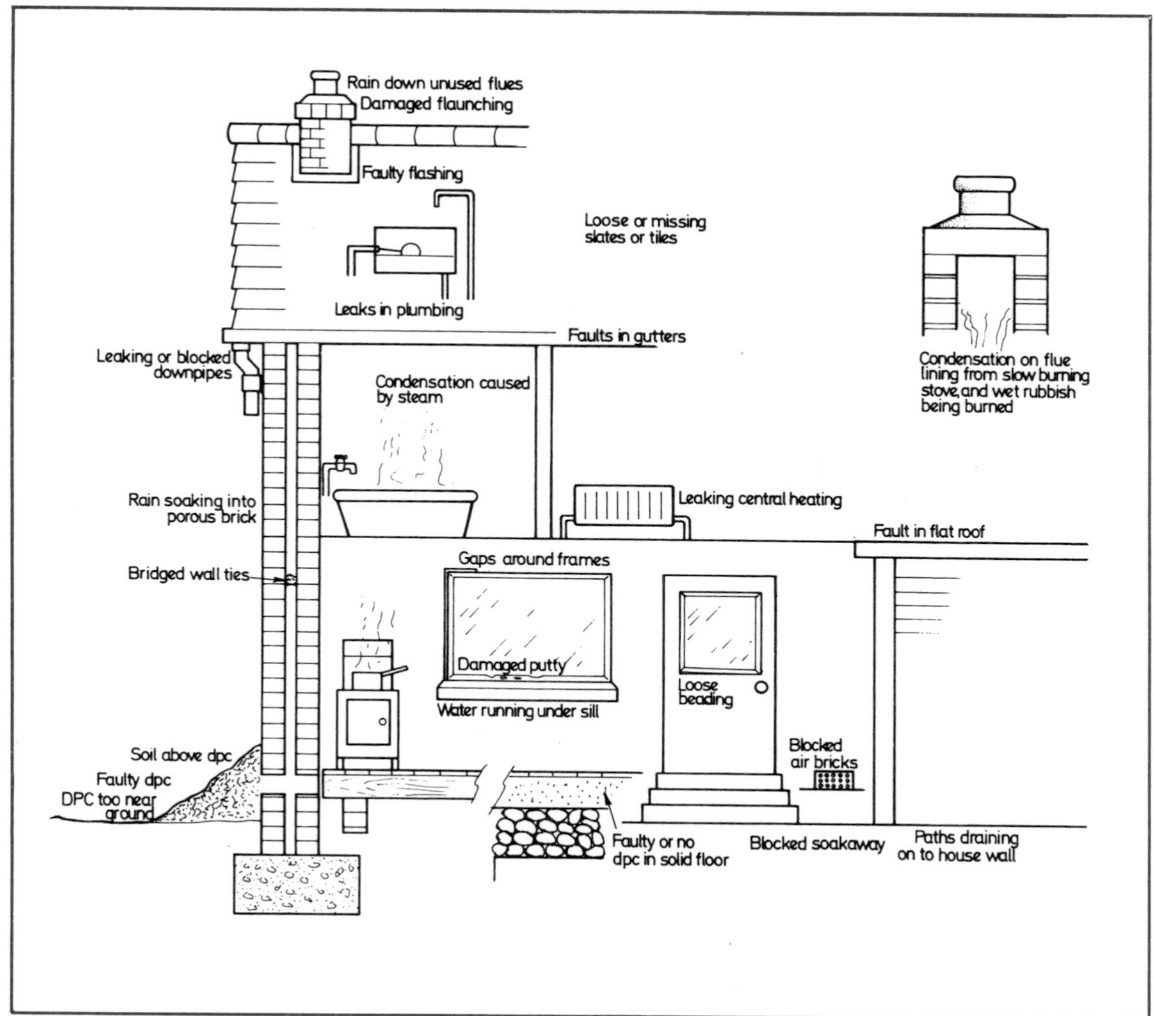

Where damp is most likely to attack your home

then, as the lost heat kept the flue warm. Nowadays, when boilers are far more efficient and therefore lose for less heat up the chimney, you can get gases condensing on the cold flue, causing staining and damage to the flue lining.

The simplest way of adding a lining is to use a flexible metal tube connected between boiler and chimney pot. However, there are certain fuels which attack even this type of lining, so it is wise to check before ordering. If a flexible liner is not suitable, you will have to use salt glazed pipes, but these are far more difficult to fix in an already completed flue.

At the base of a chimney stack you will find sheet material has been used to seal the joint between the roof and the stack. This is called a flashing, and it is important that it is in good condition. The most common material used is lead but, in some modern houses, you may find a fibrous sheeting has been used instead. Very often the mortar holding the flashing cracks away. This, of course, needs making good, and any gaps in the flashing need sealing with a mastic.

Now move down to gutter level. Again, you will often find that mortar is used to seal the gaps at the tile ends. Birds very often dig this out so they can nest in the eaves, so loose and crumbling material should be removed and new mortar applied.

Gutters and down pipes

We are now in a position to examine the state of the gutters. This will vary considerably according to the age of the house and its location. Ensure that there are no holes in the gutter, and that water can flow freely to the down pipes. You can test these points by taking a can of water to the point farthest from a down pipe and feeding the water into the gutter, and watching how it flows.

The water may flow sluggishly due to silt off the tiles, and in rural areas the gutters can soon become choked with leaves, old nests and other debris. All this must, of course be removed, and it pays to have regular checking sessions, with the most important one after the leaves have fallen off the trees.

To discourage birds, fit a wire or plastic cage in the top of each down pipe. If you are troubled with leaves, fit a plastic mesh guard over the gutter to keep them out.

If water finds a way out of the gutter other than the down pipe, it may saturate a wall area. If you are unlucky, this may find a way to the internal leaf of the wall and you will find damp patches in the adjacent bedroom.

You may also have noticed when doing the water check that water gathers in certain spots, indicating that the gutter has sagged at this point. The usual cause is a faulty gutter bracket. The actual bracket may be damaged, or the holding screws may have rusted in the board into which they are screwed.

Down pipes rarely give trouble, though they may become blocked if birds are given the chance to nest in the tops. With the old cast iron type, you will see that there are gaps between each pipe section where one pipe fits into another. It is wise not to seal these gaps, as they give you a clear indication if the pipe becomes blocked; it will always overflow at the joint immediately above the blockage. If the joints are sealed, the water must overflow at gutter level.

Very often you can clear nest debris by feeding a garden hose in the top of the pipe, turning on the water and pushing the hose down. A note of warning, however—do not wear your best clothes for this job! If the blockage really is serious, you can hire a flexible drain clearing tool of the type operated by a hand drill. It is easy to use and very effective.

Checking rainwater gutters. Do it regularly

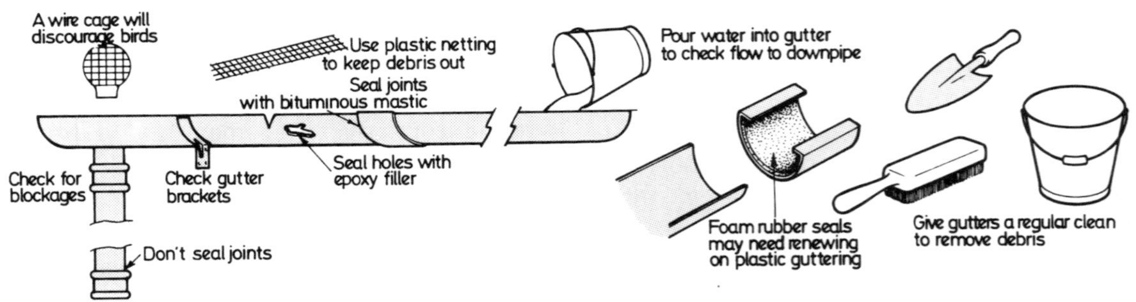

Walls

Next, examine the walls. It is not often realised that brick walls are designed to absorb a certain amount of water without any ill effects. This latter evaporates as the weather dries. Where the bricks are too porous, or where the pointing between them is crumbling, rain may penetrate too far.

With a properly constructed cavity wall, this penetration may still have little effect other than to cool down the wall too much. If any of the wall ties are bridged by mortar, due to poor workmanship, the moisture will pass across into the inner leaf of the wall and appear as damp patches indoors. You cannot reach the wall ties, but you can seal the outer brick wall to prevent damp getting in.

First you need to re-point the brickwork wherever you find the mortar soft and crumbling. Then treat the wall with a silicone water repellent fluid, flooding it on to the wall so that it completely coats the outer face of the brick. Try to keep it off window frames, porch roofs and glass, for although transparent, it forms a skin of silicone which is just about impossible to move. Cracks and gaps in any wall rendering need to be sealed, and you can find details of this in chapter 6.

About 150 mm (6 in) up from the ground, at the base of your walls, you should find a horizontal layer set in the brickwork. This is the damp-proof course, and it may take the form of a bitumen strip, pieces of slate or special impervious bricks, all of which will be referred to as the dpc. This is designed to prevent damp climbing up into the brickwork from the earth below, and to do this it must of course be continuous and unbroken. Should the dpc become bridged in any way water may find its way into the house at skirting board level, resulting in damp patches, ruined decorations, and possibly wood rot.

In an old house, there may be no damp proof course, but just a very thick wall, relying on its sheer bulk to keep the damp at bay. Very often it can, but where paths have been built up close against the wall, or earth is piled against it, you may find that the wall shows signs of retaining the damp.

Putting in a damp-proof course (dpc)

Where a damp-proof course is faulty, or does not exist, there are two courses of action. First, you can employ a reputable company to do the work of inserting a damp-proof barrier, or, second, you can tackle the job yourself. Let us look at these options.

Electro-osmosis is a specialist professional treatment that is being phased out. The work involves setting a copper strip in the wall, then connecting it to a special earthing terminal sunk deep into the ground. The effect is to earth out the electrical potential inherent in each droplet of water rising by capillary action in the wall. For some reason which no one seems to understand, it reverses the flow of droplets and water is in fact driven down, not up. Given time, the wall will dry out. With this method you receive a guarantee assuring you that the trouble will not recur.

Another approach is to sink tubes into the wall, to which are connected bottles containing a damp-resisting liquid. The liquid is gravity-fed into the wall, where it forms a barrier against rising damp. Yet another system consists of small drainage tubes set into the wall, angled down so that moisture drains off with a syphonic action. There are also firms who saw through a horizontal mortar joint, inserting a new damp-proof course membrance as they go.

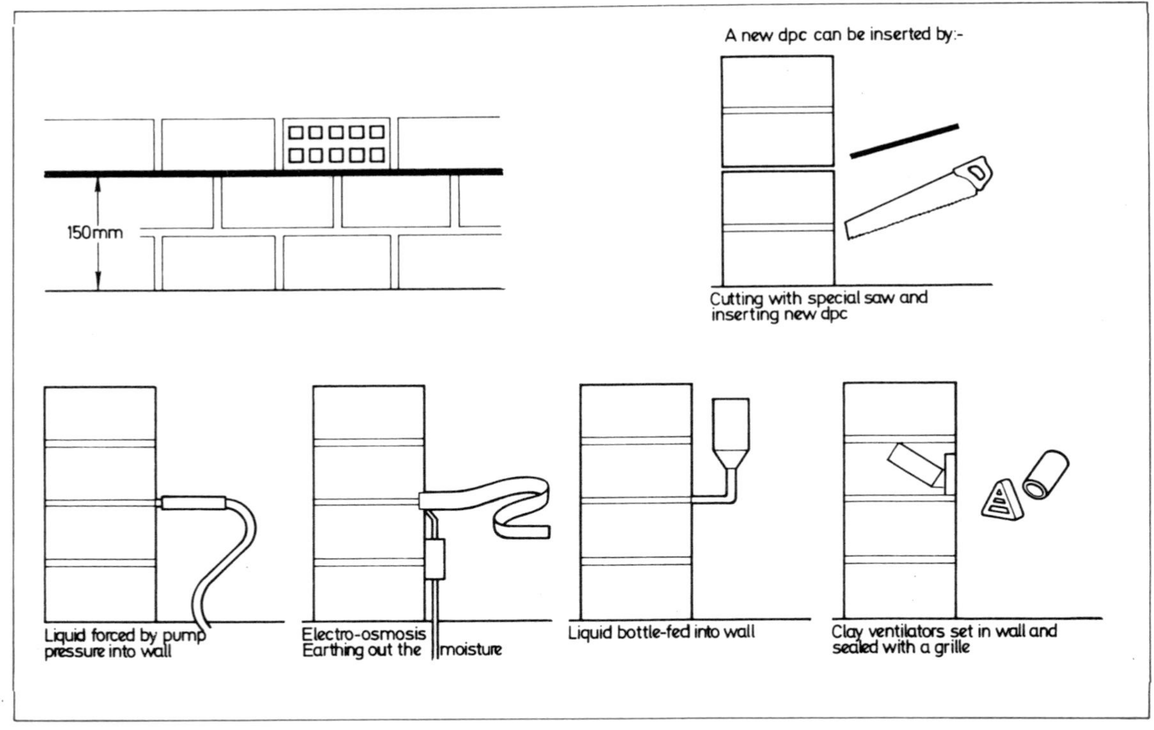

Different ways of providing a wall with a damp proof course (dpc)

If you have the work done professionally, be sure to keep the guarantee against the day you may wish to sell. If your house has had a reputation for damp, you need to have proof that the matter has been effectively dealt with.

The second option is to tackle the work yourself, and this is possible without too much trouble. There is a specialist company willing to supply the know-how and the necessary damp resisting liquid to anyone willing to do the actual work. The fluid is gravity-fed into the walls through holes bored in them, and it will form a barrier through which the damp cannot pass. Once completed, the company offer a 20 year guarantee against further trouble in the area treated.

I think this is the ideal solution for young couples with limited financial resources buying their first home where they have to put right damp problems. If you are involved with a building society, check first that they accept the system. I have found at least one society which will not.

Many building societies are sensitive concerning the subject of damp, probably because of the considerable structural damage that neglected damp can cause. For this reason, some insist that the remedial work be done by a specialist company offering a twenty or thirty year guarantee, and some offer a shortlist of companies they would like you to deal with.

There is little room for discussion in such cases, as the advance from the building society will be conditional on satisfactory completion of the damp treatment.

Hire shops can give assistance, as certain shops now stock a unit which dispenses damp-resisting liquid under pressure so that is can be forced into the wall. This greatly speeds up the process, as gravity-feed is a slow business.

The damp-resisting liquid which is pump-applied can also be used for sealing off areas affected by damp—other than defective damp proof courses. The liquid is useful around window frames, and particularly window ledges, to make the masonry impervious to water. This process should not be confused with a silicone water repellent which is a surface treatment only. The latter does not protect in depth.

Flat roofs

Flat roofs to porches, garages or extensions can be a real headache as far as damp penetration is concerned, for moisture lying on a flat surface has an excellent chance of percolating through at some weak point. Treatments for flat roof areas can be found in chapter 5.

Door and window frames

However well door and window frames fit when first installed, wood tends to shrink with age, allowing gaps to form between the frame and the adjoining masonry. This will allow water to get in—especially on aspects where the wind plays on the wall. Water may then be under pressure, and it will seep in. The damage it may do to timberwork has already been mentioned in chapter 3, but if it penetrates to the inner surface of the wall, it can also cause stains on your wallcoverings—or it may actually push them off. The use of vinyl will have little effect against attack from the rear—except perhaps to hide the trouble until a more advanced stage of attack.

Seal all gaps in the frames with mastic. You can use strips for small gaps, or a tubed mastic or mastic from a cartridge for the larger gaps. Do not use cement mortar or putty, as both these materials harden with age, in which case the cracks will open again.

Do not ignore damaged putty in frames, as damp may seep into the frame, causing rot in timber and rust in metal. Both of these problems are dealt with in chapters 3 and 4. Also check the bases of exterior doors, as rain may be driven in under wind pressure, soaking mats or carpets. The simplest solution here is to fit a weather bar which will keep the water out. There are a number of designs, but basically you have interlocking mouldings which come together when the door is closed, directing water into an outer groove from which it can drain away. Choose a type which offers the least obstruction at floor level to avoid the possibility of someone tripping over it.

Drainage from paths and drives

The only exterior damp problem worth mentioning is that of drainage from paths and drives and, in severe cases, from land. This will depend entirely on the location of the house, but if the house is situated in a hollow, it must be well drained. If water tends to drain off the land, seek the advice of your borough surveyor concerning the possibility of land drains—porous piping which can collect and lead away surface water.

Ensure that paths drain away from house walls and that any new paths are cambered with a convex surface to drain off water. Patios should have drainage holes if all the joints have been pointed. Down pipes which are not connected to a drainage system should have a suitable soakaway nearby to absorb excessive amounts of water. In most areas you are not permitted to drain rainwater into the normal drainage system; it is just not built to cope with floodwater, and in freak storms you can end up with water pressure lifting manholes and distributing sewage into gardens and roads.

Check to see the little walls around gulleys are unbroken. These allow for a degree of back-flooding without the water coming over the top. If you remove the little wall, there can be flooding if the drains block.

Interior damp

You will encounter two main forms of internal damp and many people still find it hard to distinguish one from the other. First there is structural damp, where you will see the effects internally of some of the problems we discussed outside—blocked gutters and down pipes, damage to the roof, porous walls, gaps around windows and doors, faulty dpc.

All of these problems appear during spells of wet weather and this is really the time to hunt for weak spots in the defences. Check the roof when the rain is really coming down heavily. Look for tell-tale rivulets down rafters, wet patches on the loft floor, and damp patches on the chimney breast where it goes out through the roof. The noise of soot dropping in blocked fireplaces, suggests that water is coming down the flue. Check also for signs of water dripping from gutters or cascading out of down pipes. With all these problems, the first priority is to seal off the entrance points from the outside. Only then can you set to and repair the inside.

The second form of damp is far more subtle, and it is caused by condensation. The general rule is that it does not occur on mild damp days; watch for it on cold, dry days. The first signs are usually on single glazed windows, where you will see the glass has steamed up. This is caused by moisture-laden air coming into contact with a cold surface and the effect is for the moisture in the air to be deposited as tiny droplets of water.

Warm air can hold considerable amounts of water vapour, which is why you may see no sign of trouble in the warmer rooms. However, when this warm air encounters a

How to clear water from paths and drives

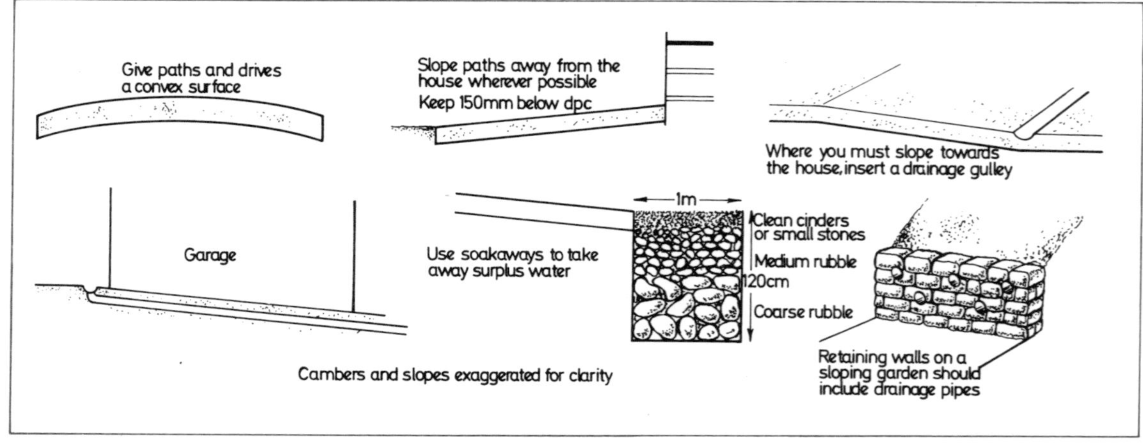

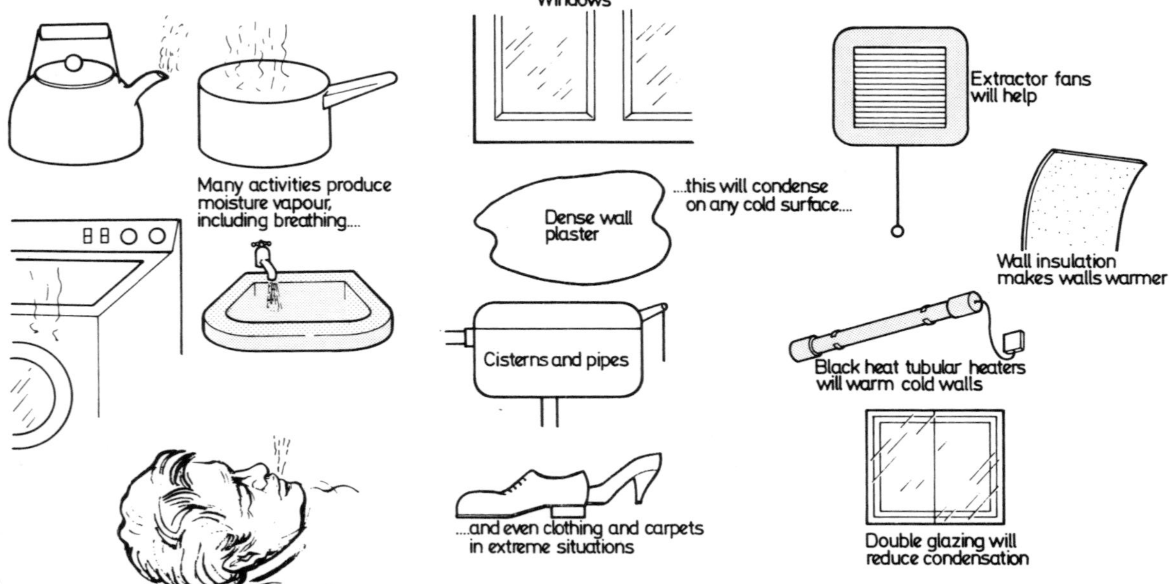

The causes and cures for condensation in the home

colder surface, then it loses the ability to hold the water vapour and you have condensation. Unfortunately glass is not the only surface affected. A cold wall will encourage condensation, which will appear as a damp patch on your decorations. North facing walls, or walls exposed to winds will be most affected and also areas which are badly ventilated, such as behind a wardrobe or chest of drawers.

These patches are often mistaken for structural damp, so if you spot them on a cold, dry day—suspect condensation!

Preventing damp by double-glazing

Double glazing helps cure the problem on windows, for the air trapped between the two panes of glass keeps the inner face warm and less likely to encourage condensation. With some d-i-y systems, condensation forms between the panes of glass. This does not happen with factory-sealed units, because a dry gas is inserted during manufacture, but it may apply to some home-installed systems.

For this reason it is wise to install a system where you can get at the interior in some way for an occasional wipe over of the surfaces. You can make frames removable; to hinge open or to slide. It does not really matter as long as you have access. Do not seal the frames with putty or mastic, for you may well trap enough damp air between frames to give misting when the sun comes out. This time you will not be able to get at it!

One trick for reducing the problem is to drill fine holes from the centre air gap through to the outside air, angling the holes down so no water can pass up. The theory is that outside cold air during winter is far drier than the air inside your house, so the gap will keep dry through fine ventilation.

Making walls warmer

Walls can be made warmer by cavity infill—the system done by professional operators

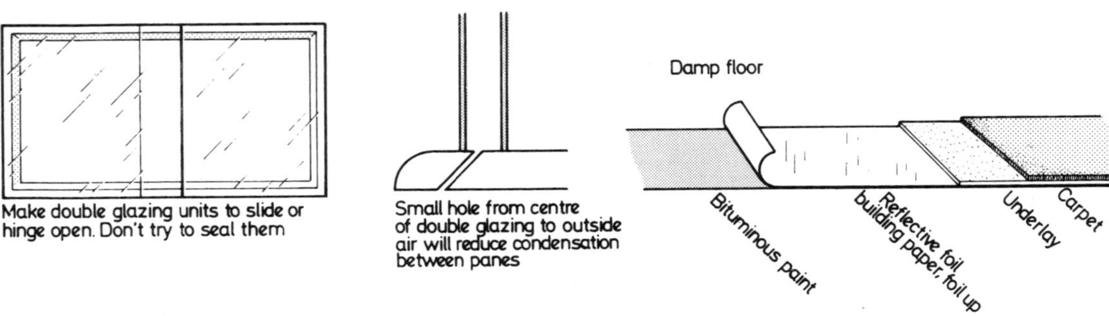

Centre, how to reduce condensation in your double glazing. Right, a way of stopping damp rising through a floor

to improve the wall insulation. Once a house has been treated, it is rare that condensation appears on the wall. Note, however, that if the air is still full of moisture it will try to find somewhere to condense. If only windows are double glazed, you may then find more damp on exposed walls. If the walls are cavity filled, you may, in severe cases, find moisture on carpets situated on cold floors; on shoes and clothing in wardrobes, and on cold lavatory cisterns and basins. It seems impossible to win!

Another way of treating walls is to line the inside face with an expanded polystyrene veneer stuck on with a special adhesive. You can then decorate over the top. The wall will be warmer to the touch after treatment and far less likely to encourage condensation.

Added warmth can be achieved by fitting a black heat tubular heater on particularly cold wall surfaces. Fix the heater at the base of the wall and it will give just enough warmth to keep the chill off the surface. Rated at only 60 to 80 watts to the foot it is not expensive to run.

Where damp is actually striking through a wall from outside, the expanded polystyrene material is of no value. In fact it will be pushed off the wall as the damp attacks the adhesive holding it. The best treatment is to seal off the wall from outside, but where this proves impossible due to access—as with a basement area—you can buy special damp-resisting lining material by the roll which will hold back the damp. This is stuck to the wall. There is also a damp-resisting coating which can be brush applied, and this too forms a damp-resisting skin which holds back the moisture. It in no way cures the fault.

The above methods are not, in my opinion, the ideal solutions, for there is always the danger that damp, when it is unable to escape, may climb higher up the house and come out in rooms so far not affected.

Treating damp walls

In basement areas, and other areas where the walls are in poor condition due to damp, you can buy a special corrugated wall surfacing material called a lath. This is fixed to the wall, after which its corrugated surface forms the ideal surface for replastering. Once treated, no further damp can get through. Such treatment can make a damp basement habitable in a very short time.

When it comes to decorating walls in potentially damp areas, there are special anti-condensation paints available. These resemble emulsion paint, but they have the ability to absorb a certain amount of moisture, allowing it to evaporate off later. These paints also contain a fungicide which discourages mould growth. Remember that ceiling tiles of expanded polystyrene or fibre board will make the surface warmer, discouraging condensation. If you wish to decorate such tiles, the ideal time is before you put them up; it is much easier.

We have touched on remedial measures, but by far the best action is to find ways of reducing the moisture content of the air. Extractor fans in kitchen and bathroom will help—coupled with keeping these doors closed while steam is being produced. Invisible steam in a warm room will quickly pass to colder rooms, given the chance, so steam from a warm bathroom may appear as damp patches on the wall of the spare bedroom.

One of the results of condensation on paintwork and wallcoverings is the growth of fine moulds which cause staining. This problem has been dealt with at the end of chapter 5.

Dampness in floors

Floors may also suffer from damp. The timber floor is normally no problem, though you should make sure that air bricks on exterior walls are kept free at all times. Never allow these to be blocked during winter months, or you may get trouble with dry rot (see chapter 3).

The main trouble comes from solid floors where the concrete is actually sitting on the ground. If the floor is properly constructed it should include a horizontal damp-proof course which prevents moisture rising through. If this is the case, and you experience damp in cold weather, this too may be a simple case of condensation.

You can test it by building a little wall of putty or Plasticine to form a box, then pressing a piece of glass on to the wall. Press it fairly close to the floor, but not touching it. If moisture gathers on the top of the glass, this is condensation—moisture being deposited from the room. If you find moisture on the underside of the glass, this is moisture coming up through the floor—rising damp.

In most cases, the problem can be solved by treating the floor with a damp-resisting sealer. This may be an epoxy-based material or it may be bitumen-rubber based. An ideal combination is to coat the floor with a bitumen based coating, then place on it a waterproof building paper with a reflective foil face. Fix it with the foil surface up, and you have a surface which is ready to cover with underlay and carpet, or vinyl. The foil acts as a reflector, preventing room warmth being absorbed by the concrete.

There are a few severe cases where, due to the location of the house in a hollow, water comes up under pressure. This has been known to lift wood-block floors and no simple coating will prevent it. If you find you have persistent damp in a floor and you live in an area with high ground around you, seek the advice of your borough surveyor. You may need land drainage to take the water away.

If the moisture is a case of condensation, a reflective building paper, followed by underlay and carpet, or a foam-backed vinyl, should solve the problem. A solid sheet vinyl on its own may not be enough and you may find moisture from condensation between floor and vinyl.

Another offender is the old quarry tiled floor. This can be very cold to the touch, and you may find condensation on floorcoverings. A simple solution, if you do not mind losing the tiles, is to cover the floor with a screeding compound. This is a self-levelling cement-based material which will produce a new surface on which to lay your covering, and it will not be so prone to condensation. It is also an ideal way of levelling uneven floors such as old quarries. No floorcovering will last long on a rough, uneven floor.

Checking for water leakage

Apart from the two main causes of damp already discussed, it is wise to keep a regular check on all areas where water is involved in one way or another.

Look for leaking pipes under sinks and basins where a joint may have loosened. Feel around the points where pipes go below floorcoverings—especially where you have vinyl on the floor. The old linoleum floorcoverings used to break up if subjected to continuous damp, and that in itself was an indication of trouble. Today, vinyls, being impervious to water, will show no external signs of damp though the floorboards below may be saturated.

Check on water closets, especially the seal between the basin and the soil pipe. As mentioned earlier, slight damp may just be condensation, but a bad seal can cause more permanent damage. Make sure central heating pipes are tight at the joints. Capillary soldered joints do not give trouble, but compression joints may need occasional tightening.

See that pressed steel radiators are not leaking. The old cast iron radiators were ugly, but would last for ever. Modern steel ones are very thin and can be attacked from within. You can combat this by inserting an anti-corrosion fluid in the system either as soon as the central heating is installed or after draining down and refilling. The liquid can be inserted by pouring into the expansion tank, then draining water off at the drain cock on the boiler so the water in the tank is drawn into the system.

If you find small pinhole leaks, there is a liquid sealer which can be added to the central heating system to seal off the holes from inside. It is important to catch trouble early or you will have to replace the radiators.

Check the hot water cylinder in the airing cupboard and see that there are no leaks. The older type tanks of galvanised iron with the circular inspection plate should be checked externally for signs of rusting or leaking at joints. The water storage tank (or tanks) in the loft should be examined for corrosion. If you have the galvanised iron type of tank, drain it off every three or four years and examine the inside for rusting. A coat of special tasteless bituminous paint every few years will ensure that the tank stays in good condition.

If you are replacing a tank, a polythene one will give far less trouble as it is unaffected by rust or corrosion. The only point to remember is that it is a more delicate piece of equipment. Never hoist yourself into the loft by pipes connected to the tank—or you may get very wet!

Frost-protection is of course a precautionary measure against damp and it is wise to ensure that all exposed pipes are well lagged, including expansion pipes and waste pipes. This is particularly important when a roof area has been well insulated, because the waste heat from downstairs which used to keep the chill off the loft is no longer available, so the loft space will be that much colder.

Chapter 7 Repairs at roof level

The roof is without doubt the most difficult area you will have to deal with, and if you are in any way worried by heights, keep off it. If you do venture on, be sure to use the proper means of access. As previously mentioned you will need a ladder which extends at least three rungs above gutter height at the point at which you are working, and a roof ladder of the type which hooks over the ridge.

Make sure the ladder cannot slip, and be particularly careful when resting it on plastic guttering. This is far more slippery than metal. It is quite strong enough to take the weight, but it would be wise to put a ring bolt into the fascia board (to which the gutters are fixed) and then run a cord from the ring to the ladder rung. This will give you a sound footing when stepping back on the ladder from the roof ladder.

The main thing to check for on the roof is weak points where the rain could find a way into the house. The effects of damp have already been dealt with in detail in chapter 6. As suggested in that chapter, it is a good idea to check from inside during heavy rain. This will give you a guide as to where exterior repairs may be needed. It is not always easy to pinpoint the source of trouble, for water may trickle in rivulets down a rafter or along the roof felting before dripping off and becoming visible.

Tiles

Start at the top of the roof with the ridge tiles; these may be loose due to frost action. Lift off loose ones and chip away all loose or soft mortar, then make up a new mortar of 1 cement to 7 or 8 soft sand plus a plasticiser.

Dealing with gaps in roofing

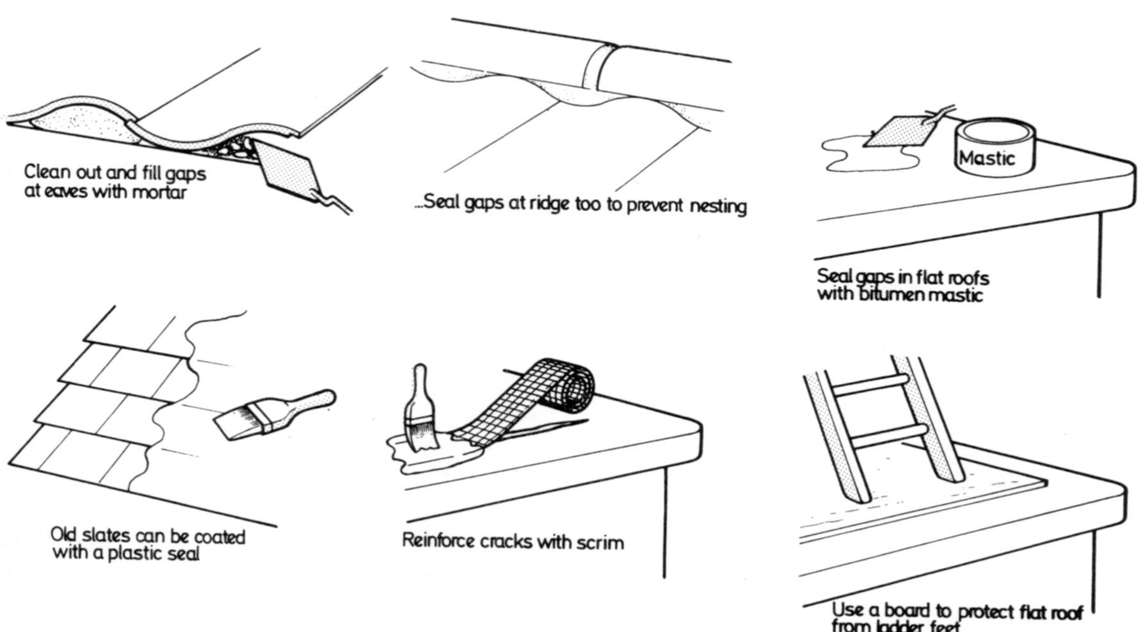

Keep the mortar mix as dry as possible so that it does not slop about and mark your tiles. Damp the ridge tiles in water and drain off before putting them back. This reduces the suction of the tiles so that they will not remove water from the mortar. Bed the tiles on the mortar and make a neat joint with a small trowel.

The same mortar mix can be used for sealing any gaps at the tile ends. Frost, and the action of birds looking for good nesting points may have removed the old mortar. Clean out any remaining mortar and brush the tiles clean with an old paintbrush kept for dusting. Then damp the holes with water and apply your dryish mix, trowelling it smooth. If birds really are a nuisance, add a little black pepper to your mix and they will not be so keen on pecking it out.

Cracks in tiles can be sealed with mortar, and to improve adhesion, you could add a little pva adhesive to the mixing water, or seal the holes with an epoxy filler. A touch of tile paint can be used to disguise the repair.

If a tile has slipped, and this is a rare occurrence unless you are dealing with an older property, it means it has lost its nibs, or the tiling batten underneath has rotted away. Very often it is a combination of rusted nails which loose a hold on the tile, plus the weight of snow or ice during a cold spell. If you find loose ones, clean the meeting faces and use an epoxy filler as an adhesive. This will bond the loose one to its neighbours.

Slates

Small cracks in slates can be sealed with the same filler, but where you meet serious gaps or breaks, use glass fibre bandage to reinforce the repair. Spread a thin layer of filler over the damaged area, lay down some bandage and press it into the filler with an old brush. Then spread another layer of filler over the top. This will give a strong repair which, even if the slate moves slightly, will not crack.

If the slates are in a generally poor condition, i.e. flaking away and slipping, you can now buy an excellent plastic coating which, when spread over the slates, forms an unbroken flexible plastic skin over the whole roof area. Where money is short, this offers an ideal alternative to having the roof stripped and re-covered. The secret is to lay the material on thick—do not try to spread it like paint.

Gutters

When you reach gutter level you may find another series of gaps in a heavily profiled roof, where the birds have pulled out the mortar and nested. Dig out all old and flaking material and re-point with the same mortar mix we used further up the roof. Again, your black pepper will discourage birds.

Check that the gutter brackets are anchored securely to the fascia boards. In older houses, the board may have become soft through rot so that screws lose their grip; or the screws themselves may have rusted away until they no longer grip. In the first case it will be necessary to remove the guttering and brackets from the damaged area, take down the fascia board and put up new board. As you have the opportunity, prime and paint the new board before you put it up. It is much easier.

Be warned that if you are taking down cast iron guttering it is extremely heavy—you will need some help. A simple pulley and rope system with the rope lashed to the guttering will make lowering easier. Never take a chance on your own!

If only the screws have failed, remove the gutter sections, plug the holes in the fascia board with mastic or exterior grade stopping and re-position the brackets. Remember that your gutter must have a steady fall towards the down pipe, at least 25 mm (1 in) in every 3 m (9 ft). This is best marked out with a string line and pins before you start fixing brackets, or you may find you run out of fascia board before you get to the end!

Check the gutter lengths for rusting, or for gaps between sections. Rust should be removed back to bright metal, then the area treated with a rust inhibitor before you fill the damage with epoxy filler. Get it to a nice smooth finish by rubbing with emery when hard to ensure there are no snags to hold debris. Joints, where there may be slight movement, can be sealed with a bitumen mastic trowelled into the gap. Again make sure it has a smooth finish.

Where guttering is in a bad way and is not strong enough to refit, get one of the modern plastic systems. They are far easier to handle because the sections are so much lighter; one person can fit a full length. Once installed, plastic gutters are self-cleaning and need no painting. By the way, remember to paint your fascia boards before putting up new guttering. You can't use a blowlamp near plastic gutter brackets, gutters or down pipes.

You will find sections of guttering merely clip together, bedding down on a special foam gasket. Down pipe sections are usually welded together with a special cement.

Chimney stacks

Before leaving roof level, have a look at the chimney stacks. Any pots should be bedded on mortar, called 'flaunching', and if this is damaged, the old mortar should be chipped away and new mortar applied. Cracks and gaps in otherwise sound mortar can be filled with a mortar mix to which has been added some pva adhesive to increase adhesion.

Check also the pointing between the bricks. If this is crumbling, dig it out to a depth of about 12 mm (½ in), brush the joints clean and re-point with a mortar. You can buy this as a dry mix in bags, and

Dealing with a chimney stack—and how to get to it safely

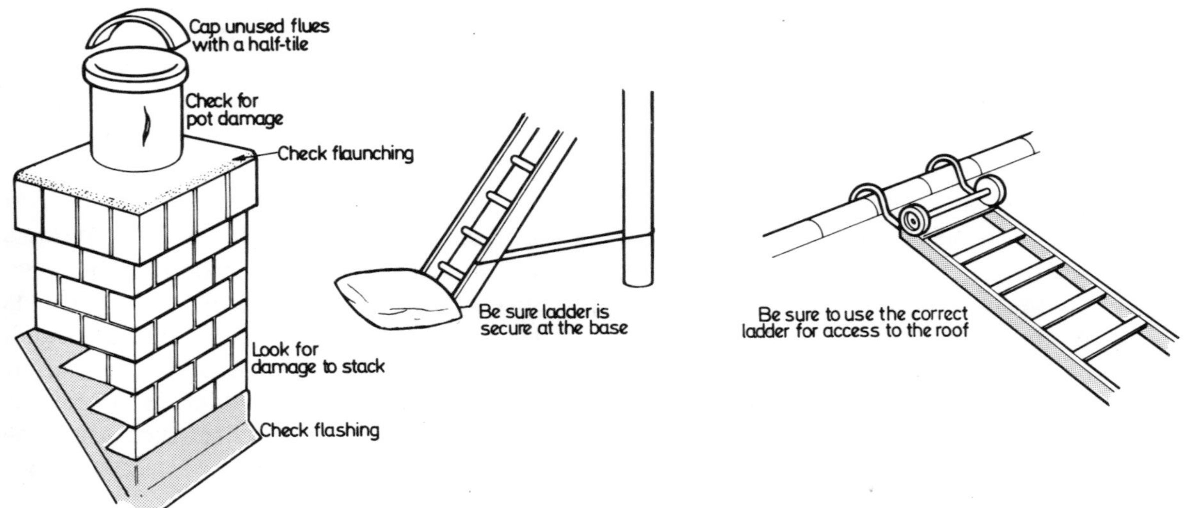

all you need is to add water. Again, be sure to keep the mix really dry or you will mark your brickwork. Damp the joints before you fill them with clean water applied with an old paintbrush. This stops the bricks sucking water from your new mortar and weakening it.

If you find the stack is in poor shape, with bad cracking and perhaps deformation of the stack, this is probably caused by damage coming through from the inside. For this job you would be wise to call in professional help because of the weight of material involved. A scaffold will have to be erected around the stack while it is dismantled and rebuilt.

At the base of the stack you will find the joint between stack and roof slates or tiles. This is called the 'flashing', and it should be examined to see there are no gaps or cracks. Sometimes the flashing works away from the joints in the stack, in which case you need to dig out the old mortar, brush the gaps clean, push the flashing back in place and secure it with scraps of lead used as wedges. Then re-point as with the rest of the stack. If it is loose at the roof side, lift the flashing, brush on a liberal coat of bituminous mastic and press the flashing on to it.

Flat roofs

Flat roof areas often create a problem because water frequently seems to find a way in. Basically this is because the water may not drain off, but just lies on the roofing in pools, seeping into the smallest cracks.

The most common covering material is bituminous sheeting, very often covered with a layer of fine stones. If you can find definite cracks, clean them out, then fill the cracks with bituminous mastic applied with a small trowel. Where there are tears, or the cracking is quite severe, strengthen the repair with a hessian bandage. Apply a layer of mastic, press the hessian into it until well bedded down, then apply a further layer of bitumen.

Where a roof is in bad shape, brush it clean, then apply a plastic roofing compound, laying it on thick. This will set to a tough unbroken skin, giving you a brand new surface. Pay particular attention to flashings, where they are set into brickwork and then taken on to the roof. This is a very weak spot, and mastic should be used in preference to mortar. Should there be slight movement, the mastic can take it.

Lean-to glass roofs

Lean-to roofs always present a problem—first of access, then of keeping clean, for dirt and moss growth soon spoil a clear surface. Where possible it is a good idea to have an opening panel in the roof so that a ladder can be put through. Failing this you will need scaffold boards rested across the joists to give you safe access. Never risk walking across the glass, even when wired.

A weak solution of caustic soda will remove most glass grime, but protect your hands with rubber gloves, and your eyes with safety glasses. Where you think water may be getting in at the glazing bars, clean off any dust and dirt, then seal the bars with mastic glazing tape, pressing it well into the corners. The easiest to handle has a foil face and this also looks neater and prevents the mastic drying out.

Corrugated plastic sheeting is best cleaned with water and liquid detergent. Do not use an abrasive. If grime has got between sheets, you will have to remove the sheets and scrub them clean with a soft scrubbing brush and detergent. There is a transparent glazing tape available which is useful for sealing gaps likely to collect dirt. The tape is waterproof, providing it is applied to a clean, dust-free, dry surface.

Chapter 8 Outside jobs

The two main materials encountered on outside work are timber and concrete, and you will find it useful to refer to chapter 3 in addition to the information given in this chapter. Timber will be affected by damp, and concrete, while durable, is weakened by the attack of frost during winter months. Water seeps into cracks, freezes and expands, applying very considerable pressure to the concrete, causing flaking and splitting.

Fence and gate posts

Timber posts are the most vulnerable, particularly the section below ground level where perhaps water has gathered and rotted the bases. A common culprit is a concrete housing; this is where a post has been positioned, then the hole filled with concrete. This certainly gives an initially strong support, but when the post shrinks slightly, water can seep down into the concrete where it is held in contact with the timber. This inevitably leads to rotting and loosening of the post and then you have a real job releasing it. The illustration shows a way of applying leverage to lift the post free—after which the concrete will have to be removed.

If new timber posts are to be put into the ground, be sure they are well soaked in preservative—especially into the end grain. Then stand the base on rubble to ensure good drainage and fill in with earth. You will get far less trouble this way and it is not so hard to get the post out should the need arise.

By far the best way to erect timber posts is to use concrete spurs. The spur is cemented into the ground and the timber post bolted to it. This means that the timber never comes into contact with the ground at all. It is also a good idea to cap the top of each post with a piece of zinc or aluminium. Angle the top to shed the water, then pin the sheeting in place with alloy nails. Very often you will find that the end of a post is the first to begin to rot as water seeps into it.

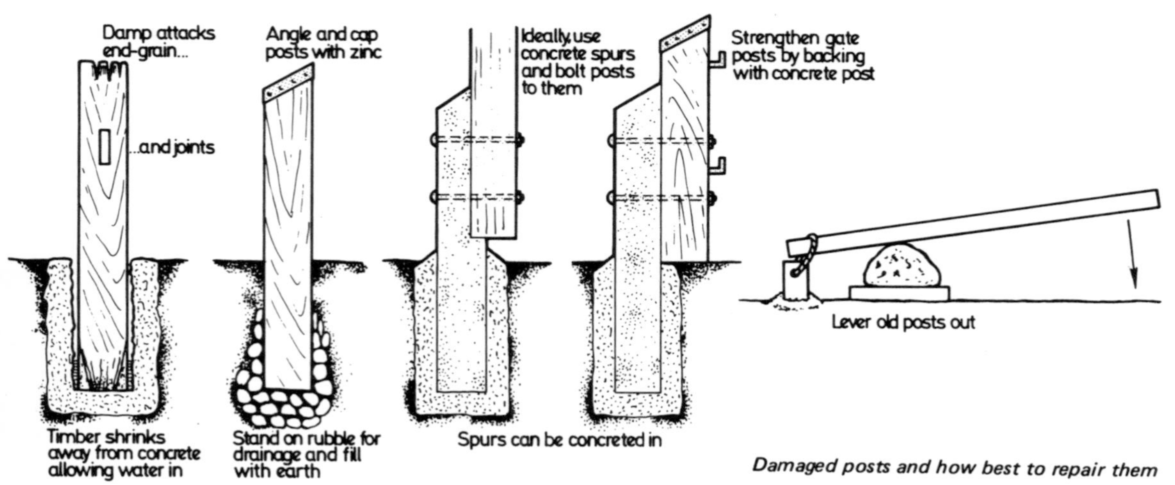

Damaged posts and how best to repair them

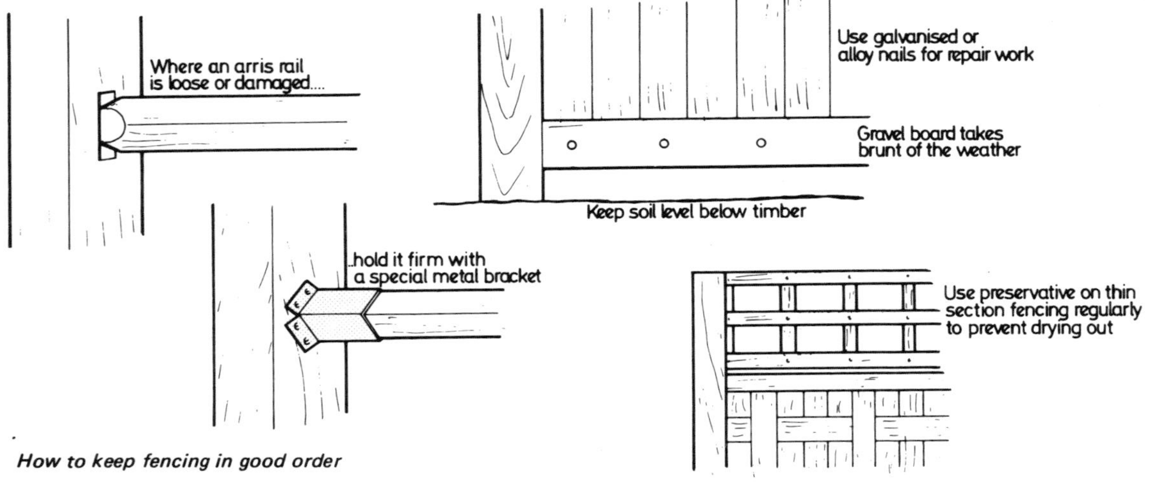

How to keep fencing in good order

As has been mentioned for other timber-work, it pays to buy pressure-impregnated wood which will be unaffected by damp or insect attack. You will see it widely used for motorway fencing.

Gate posts also present a problem because of the strain on the post holding the gate; especially if children use the gate as a swing! Where a post is loose, try to sink a concrete post behind it then bolt the timber post to it. The concrete post can then be set in concrete to give maximum support. You can get a permanent concrete stain to tone down the post to match the adjacent timber.

Timber gates also suffer from shrinkage, loosening up the joints. If you encounter this problem, take off the gate and, after numbering the joints, tap the gate apart using a rubber hammer. Clean off all the old glue, then re-assemble using a water-proof resin adhesive. Where there are gaps to fill you can use an epoxy filler, forcing the joint into a surplus of filler, then trimming off what is not needed. If you have to use screws or nails, use aluminium alloy which does not rust or stain your timber. Never try to re-assemble rotting sections; cut out all rotting timber and replace it with new.

Fencing

Arris rails, supporting fencing boards, often rot where the rail enters the recess in the timber or concrete post. The simplest way of tackling this problem is to buy special rail repair brackets which act as supports for the damaged rail. The bracket can be screwed to the timber post, but with concrete ones you will need to drill and plug. If you find drilling into the post heavy going with a standard power tool and masonry drill, borrow a hammer action drill. It will make the job much easier.

When repairing fencing, make sure that the soil level is well below your fencing boards, otherwise damp will climb into the wood, probably rotting it. Some fences incorporate a special rail along the base of the fence which takes the brunt of any wetting or build-up of soil. If it becomes damaged, it can be removed and a new rail fixed in place, preferably with rustless screws.

If feather-edge boards are neglected, the thinnest sections will tend to curl, causing gaps to open in the fencing. To improve matters, choose a period of dry weather and thoroughly soak the fencing with water until the boards are pliable enough to be eased flat. Now use alloy nails to nail the boards flat. If you have to work near the edges of boards, use oval nails, or take the trouble to drill holes through the boards into which the nails can be driven. It may sound a lot of extra trouble, but it will ensure that you do not split your boards.

When the fence has dried out, give it two liberal coats of a good wood preservative. Then repeat the treatment whenever the wood starts to look dry and 'thirsty'. Choose a dry period to apply the preservative with an old paintbrush, it will not soak far into wet timber.

The thinner the sections of timber, the more treatment they seem to need—as with woven fencing panels and trellis. Give these regular treatment with a wood preservative to keep them in good condition. The wood should never be allowed to really dry out. Where material like trellis comes into close contact with greenery, there is a special grade of preservative which will not harm plant life. Many normal grades of preservative will kill plants if they come into contact before the timber has really dried off.

Sheds, garages and workshops

Timber sheds, garages and workshops also need regular treatment if the wood is to stay in good condition. Gloss paint can be used, but I always feel this is the last resort because it hides the natural beauty of the wood. If you inherit a painted structure, then treat it as any other painted surface and keep it in good condition. The important point is to ensure that the paint gets into all cracks and joints, for these are the weak points in the system. If the damp can get behind a paint film, it will soon push it off.

The normal method of decorating is to use a wood preservative, and while the accepted colour is light or dark brown, you can now get a whole range of colours, from yellow through to black. These pigmented preservatives can look most attractive, and there is no reason now why a garden room should not have orange walls with a green door—yet, with the grain of the wood showing through.

If you have a western red cedar building, then you will want to maintain the golden colour for which it is noted. Unfortunately the colour bleaches out with time, and you end up with a far less attractive grey. You can buy special preservatives designed to restore the colour by staining and this is

Putting new felt on a shed roof

the kind to choose for cedar. It is advisable not to wait until the timber is grey but to give regular coats while it is still golden and it will look more natural.

The garden workshop is not the cosiest of places during the winter months, and if you want to use it for storing tools and appliances, it is worth considering adding a weatherproof inner lining. You can do this very simply with a reflective foil building paper stapled or drawing-pinned between internal timbers. Have the reflective foil in, then cover over the timbers with fibre building board. Far less damp will get in after such treatment. As an alternative material, 500 gauge polythene sheeting could be used, stapled or pinned.

Western red cedar is a very soft wood, and nails will not get a good grip. So if you find beading or cladding coming away, replace the pieces with ring nails. These get a far better hold on the timber, and they will not pull out.

While checking outbuildings, examine the roof covering. It is probably bitumen roofing felt held with large head clout nails and perhaps reinforced with battens to hold it firm in high winds. Small tears can be sealed with a bituminous mastic and overlapped joints which are lifting can be stuck down using the mastic as an adhesive.

Where the roof covering has hardened with age and is cracking, it needs replacing. Rip it all off and burn it. Examine the roof timbers to see they are sound, then treat them with a liberal coating of preservative and allow it to dry out. You will find that modern preservatives are much faster drying than the older creosotes.

Buy a good heavy gauge roofing felt and unroll it before use. Let it stretch and flatten before you fix it. Then start at the eaves, lay strips horizontally and secure with clout nails. Place the nails so that a generous overlap of felt covers them when the next piece goes down. To get a really good seal, use bituminous mastic as an adhesive between pieces of felt. Continue until you reach the ridge, then tackle the other side if you have two sloping faces. The last piece to go on is a ridge piece—preferably stuck down.

Battens can be added to anchor the roof, but do not use too heavy gauge nails, as obviously these will be making a hole in your new covering. Treat the battens with preservative before fixing and allow them to dry before nailing in place. Put a spot of mastic over each nail head to seal it to the timber.

If yours is virtually a flat roof, start at lowest point of the roof and work up. This ensures the water runs over the joints and not into them.

Concrete surrounds and paths

Now let us have a look at the concrete surrounding the house. As mentioned earlier the main problem will be caused by the action of frost causing cracking and flaking. All loose material should be chipped away then the area wire brushed (do not forget to protect your eyes).

You can buy epoxy-based repair materials for concrete, but they tend to be expensive so, for most repairs, use a mortar mix of say 1 of cement to 6 of sand, plus the addition of some pva adhesive to the mixing water. Before you apply the mix, damp the area to be repaired, allow the water to soak in, then apply a neat brush coat of pva adhesive to the cracks. Then fill with mortar.

As has already been suggested, work with a dryish mortar mix of about sand-pie consistency. A sloppy mortar will mark the surrounding concrete and be difficult to clean off. When the repair has been made and the mortar wiped level with the rest of the concrete, cover it with damp rag or sacking for a few days so that the mortar dries out slowly. Fast drying mortar will give a very weak repair.

Where the edge of a path or step has been broken away, make up a simple mould around the damaged area into which you can pour concrete. Again, the addition of pva and the brushing of the area with neat pva will ensure a good bond. Off-cuts of laminate are ideal for moulds, shiny side to the concrete. Alternatively, you can use hardboard brushed with oil or covered with polythene so the concrete will not stick. Allow three or four hours before easing the mould away, then cover the area with damp sacking and protect it for a couple of weeks until the repair is really mature.

Where paving slabs have been used for steps, and these have been damaged on corners, it may be possible to ease the slabs out and turn them so the damage is to the rear and hidden by the risers. The same applies to brick edgings. Once the damage has been repaired, a liberal coating of silicone water repellent will discourage water from soaking in. This in turn can reduce frost damage. I once stopped the disentegration of rockery stones with silicone repellent—with no effect on the plants growing around them.

Stained areas of concrete, such as the oily marks left by a parked car on a drive, can look a mess. The worst of the oil can be removed with an oil and tar remover brushed into the stain, then washed away, but you may still be left with a mark. You can disguise this by using a concrete stain over the whole drive area. A reasonable black stain is available. Also have a simple drip tray which can be slid under the car when it is left standing.

To enhance the appearance of dull concrete, you can now buy cold macadam materials with which to re-surface the concrete. First, after cleaning the area, a bitumen priming coat is used to ensure good adhesion, then the cold bitumen is tipped from the bag and spread with a rake. It is then rolled, keeping the roller drum wet so that it does not stick to the bitumen and pull it up. Then after rolling, fine chippings can be thrown on and rolled.

For areas of shingle, a special cold bitumen liquid is available which can be sprayed over the shingle, binding it together. The latest approach to laying bitumen and stones is to buy it by the roll ready for laying on to any clean, firm surface. A priming coat is put down to ensure good adhesion, then a backing paper is removed from the roll, and the material pressed into place, producing an instant macadam surface.

Patios and paving slabs

Patios can present a problem, especially after periods of prolonged dry weather, for paving slabs may start to rock or even subside. To re-bed a slab, lift it by carefully levering it up with a spade, tamp down hard the material underneath to form a foundation. If you find soft spots, put rubble down and tamp it into the ground, then lay five blobs of new mortar slightly higher than you know will be needed. Damp the underside of the slab and lower it back in place, keeping the pressure as even as possible. Then tap down the slab using a rubber hammer or a baulk of timber until the slab is flush with its neighbours.

Always tap around the edges of a slab. A hard knock in the centre could break it. Never use a metal hammer—the handle of a club hammer is a reasonable substitute for a rubber mallet.

While on the subject of subsidence, you may occasionally find an area of path has sunk at the joint between sections, forming a ledge over which people could trip. Thin

The sequence for laying cold macadam on a path or drive

layers of concrete are not the easiest of repairs, but you can put down a thin screed if you use the method already described, of adding pva adhesive to the water of the mortar mix, then applying a liberal coating of neat pva to the concrete to be covered.

If the surface of the conrete is very smooth, it would be wise to roughen it up with a steel chisel and club hammer before putting down your pva. Protect your eyes, and sweep up all the dust and loose material before applying the adhesive. Nothing sticks well to dust. With the surface prepared, apply your new mortar, trowelling it out and feathering it so you lose the step. You may need to tap it over with a piece of board to add light ridges so that it matches the surrounding area.

Chapter 9 Twenty common problems

Not all the problems you are likely to encounter are easily classifiable. So here are some of the most common ones. I have omitted problems concerning plumbing and electrics as these appear in the companion volumes on *'Home Plumbing'* and *'Home Electrics'* in the d-i-y series.

Removing a cracked ceramic tile

The problem is to get the tile out without spoiling surrounding tiles. Drill a hole in the centre of the tile with a glass or masonry drill. Protect your eyes with safety glasses, then lever the tile away through the centre hole, using an old screwdriver blade. Work from the centre outwards.

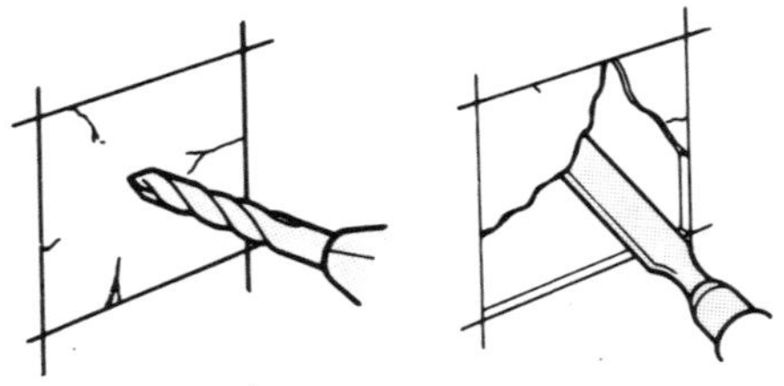

If yours is an old tile, it will be set in mortar, and it will be quite hard to move. The remaining mortar will have to be chipped away with a steel chisel and club hammer. Then apply new tile cement and stick the new tile in place.

The newer thin ceramic tiles stuck in place should be easier to move. Scrape away the remaining tile cement with an old chisel blade. If stubborn, heat the blade to soften the cement. Then apply new adhesive and fix the replacement tile. Fill the gaps with new grouting. Allow to dry, then rub away the surplus with a screwed up piece of newspaper.

Lifting damaged vinyl tiles

There is no way to get solvents at the underside of a vinyl tile, so the best approach is to use heat. Place a piece of cooking foil over the damaged tile and apply a hot iron to the foil. Keep the heat in contact until it has had time to get through to the underside, then prise up a corner of the tile and pull. It should strip away. If you are experienced with a blowtorch, this can be used as an alternative to the iron. But do be sure to keep the flame on the move so that the plastic is warmed but not melted.

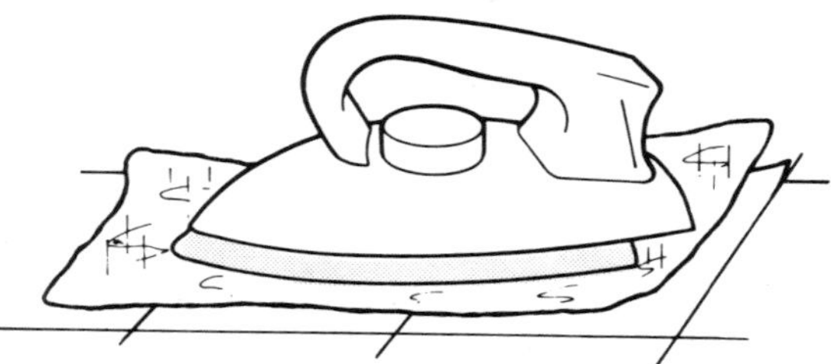

There will be a residue of adhesive, so heat a scraper and apply it to the adhesive. This should soften the adhesive enough to make it lose its grip on the floor. Solvents such as petrol very often do little more than make the adhesive very sticky, and there is a danger of fire from the fumes given off.

Having removed the old adhesive, apply fresh adhesive and fit a new matching tile. Be careful not to slide the new tile in place or you will force adhesive up between the tiles.

Easing a door lock

If a rim lock gets hard to turn, do not be tempted to squirt oil into the key hole. This can act as a collector of dust, and in a short time make the trouble even worse. Apply a little fine oil—such as you get in an aerosol spray can to the key, then place the key in the lock and turn it a few times. The oil will be sufficient to lubricate without gumming up.

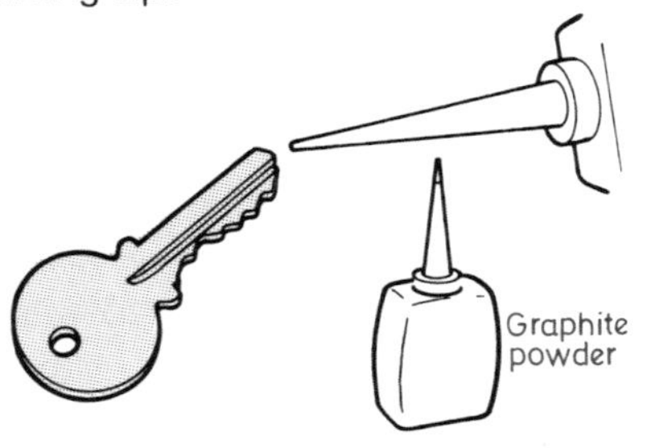

A good alternative is to use a graphite powder from a puffer pack. This is a dry lubricant which will not cause clogging. For mortice type locks, a keyhole cover is a good investment. It will prevent a through flow of air, which during dry summer months can carry a fair amount of gritty dust.

Latches and bolts which will not engage

Where a latch fails to enter a latch plate, or a bolt will not go into the securing plate, it usually means the door has dropped a shade, so the parts no longer line up. First check the door hinge at the top. A slight looseness here is sufficient to cause the trouble. If this fails, slip a piece of carbon paper between latch and plate so that when the door is closed a mark is made on the plate. Now you have the choice of filing a little from the bottom edge of the latch, or the latch plate opening—or both. Remove a little metal at a time until the door closes correctly.

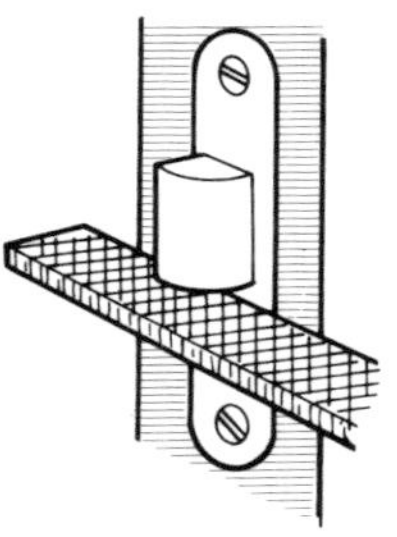

You cannot do this with a bolt. You will have to remove one part of the other—depending upon which is most convenient, plug the existing screw holes with an epoxy filler, then re-drill and screw into place. A slight tapering of the bolt tip will help to locate the tip and make it easier to close.

When you have to fit new latches or bolts, bear this problem in mind and err on the high side when fixing so that a slight drop of the door does not matter.

Loose knobs

Furniture and drawers and doors can come in for quite a bit of rough handling, and it is often the knobs which suffer. The knobs may work loose, or even pull out completely. If a timber knob pulls out, it may only be a question of applying adhesive to the wood and pressing it back in. If it is a good fit, cut a V-notch in the dowel to let the air escape; this saves all the adhesive being pushed out of the hole.

Sometimes a screw is inserted from the inside to go into the end of the dowel knob and the screw pulls away. Usually a little adhesive on a matchstick, broken in the hole and left to set is sufficient. If this is not strong enough, fill the hole with epoxy filler and push the screw into it while soft.

Where a knob has become a loose fit in a hole, line the hole with epoxy filler, cut a V-nick in the dowel of the handle and

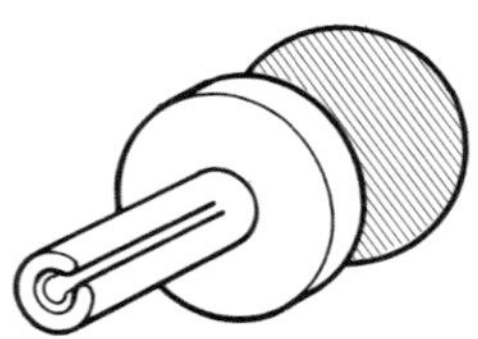

push the knob in place. Trim away surplus before it sets hard and leave to set.

In the case of ceramic knobs which have a simple screw as a means of fixing and where the hole has become enlarged, increase the hole size slightly to take a small gauge plastic wall plug. Press this in the hole and trim it flush with a craft knife, then screw the handle back in place.

Some knobs have a long bolt passing right through the drawer front and held by a nut at the rear. If the wood has worn at the rear of the drawer, remove the holding nut and slip on one or two washers, then replace and tighten the nut.

Where a wood handle has pulled away, drill holes for screws from the rear of the front piece; push in screws and press the handle against the tips to mark the exact location, then drill smaller start holes in the handle. This is essential to stop the hardwood of the handle splitting. Now screw up from the rear, after putting a touch of adhesive on the back of the handle.

Sticking drawers

This is not so much of a problem on modern furniture since the introduction of plastic slides. If you encounter older units with wood to wood slides, you may find some jamming. Examine the slides for damage. If they are badly worn it will be necessary to unscrew them and replace with new hardwood strips but, if in good condition, rub lightly with glasspaper to remove any

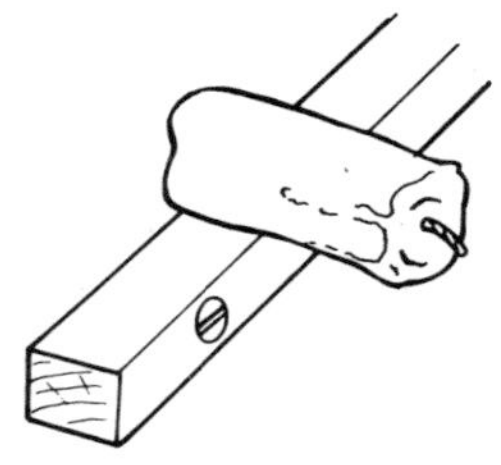

roughness. Then rub the runners with the stub of a candle which acts as an effective lubricant. You can also buy a special aerosol wood lubricant which siliconises the surface. Whichever process you choose, open drawers with care after treatment!

If you are making up new runners, line the meeting faces with off-cuts of laminate. This provides a good, hardwearing running surface. If making up new drawer systems, try to obtain the all-plastic glide systems which run much more freely.

Squeaking stairs

This can happen on both old and new properties, particularly after the installation of central heating. As timbers dry out, wedges and glues lose their hold and allow timber to move and rub against an adjoining timber area. The result is a squeak.

If you can get at the underside of the staircase, the problem is far easier to deal with. Look for the wedges holding the treads and risers in place and if loose, pull them free and remove any hardened glue. Apply new glue to the wedges and drive them back in place. When set, the squeak

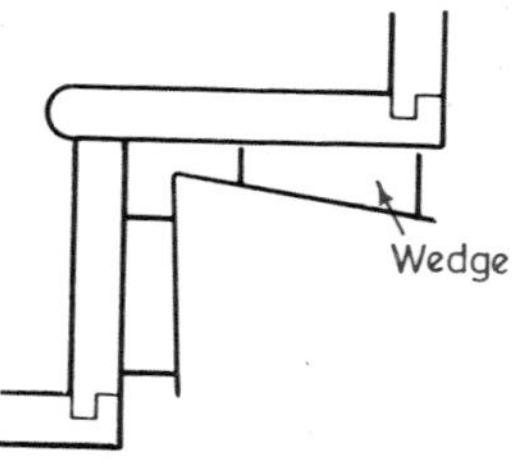

should have gone for good. A little epoxy filler pressed into gaps and cracks will be an insurance against further trouble.

Where you cannot get under the stairs, try to locate where the movement is. Cracks can be filled with epoxy filler, and treads and risers can be locked together by drilling and screwing down from riser into the tread below. Pre-drill for screws and countersink the tread so that screws go well below the wood surface. Then fill with wood stopping.

Slight squeaks can often be cured by puffing talc between gaps. This acts as a lubricant, stopping the rubbing which causes the noise.

Squeaking floorboards

Here we have the same basic problem as with the stairs, often caused by timber drying out and causing gaps. Press on the floor until you find the exact location of the squeak, then find the nearest adjoining joist. Drill the board to take the shank of a screw, countersink the board, make a start hole in the joint, then drive the screw home really tight. You should hear the board groan for the last time as the screw pulls it down tight to the joist.

Where there is no joist to screw in to, locate the exact spot where the squeak occurs, then drive a chipboard screw down between the boards. This type of screw has no plain shank, and the serrations formed by the thread tend to prevent any movement of the board. Again, a puff of talc between boards will often lubricate the area well enough to stop noise.

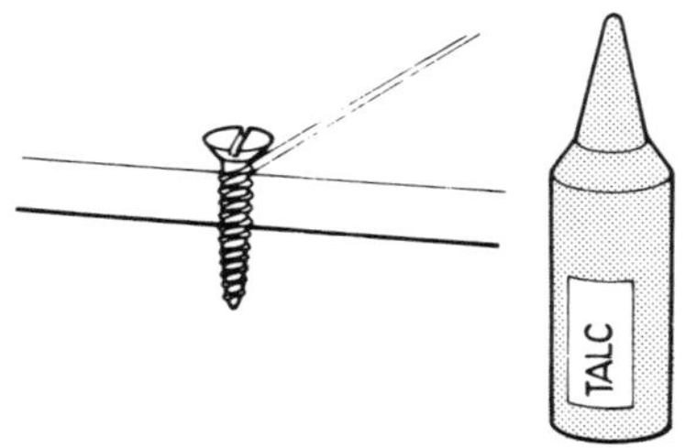

If you do encounter squeaks, deal with them before covering the floor with hardboard or plywood. These materials will not cure the trouble—in fact they could magnify the noise.

Replacing broken glass

Unfortunately there is no way of repairing cracked glass. It has to come out and be replaced by new. Assuming a pane is broken, wear thick leather gardening gloves while removing glass from a frame and use pincers to wiggle loose any obstinate pieces. With the glass out, chisel out all old putty, including the bedding putty. Use an old chisel, kept for such rough jobs, and a mallet.

A timber frame should be rubbed smooth with glasspaper, then the wood sealed with primer. A metal frame should be checked for signs of rust. Any rusted areas must be rubbed down with emery paper to remove deposits of rust, then treated with a rust inhibitor.

Measure very carefully for your new piece of glass, checking the diagonals to ensure that the pane is square. If you encounter an odd shape, such as in a front door, make a stiff paper pattern and take this with you when you order your glass. Deduct 3 mm ($^1/_8$ in) from each dimension so there is air around the glass when placed in the frame. For fairly small panes of glass, up to about 1 m (3 ft) square, use glass 3 mm thick. For larger panes of the modern picture window size, use 4 mm ($^3/_{16}$ in) and 6 mm (¼ in) for anything above this.

There are locations, such as doors and low windows, where it would be wise to install safety glass. You can now buy a laminated glass which has tremendous resistance to impact; it will shatter, but the whole piece will stay together offering no jagged edges. You would merely bounce off instead of going through! Such glass is about three times more expensive than normal glass, but the additional expenditure does offer safety and security. No thief will shatter this glass and put a hand through to release a catch.

If you wish to cut your own glass, you need a good wheel-type cutter, a straight edge and an accurate rule. Be sure to use fresh glass, because old glass will often break other than along the line. An ordinary sheet of newspaper is another excellent aid, for the rules used between columns and any horizontal lines will be extremely accurate. You can mark a very good straight line or right angle merely by laying the glass on the paper.

Experiment with your cutter before attempting to cut an accurate piece. The cutting wheel must just whisper over the glass leaving a clear score line; it must not judder or slide. With a score line made, position the glass over two or three match-sticks so the sticks run under the score, then press down either side. The glass should break clean along the cut. Small slivers can be nipped away with the square recesses on the cutter, or with pliers.

With your glass, you need linseed oil putty for timber frames, or metal casement putty for metal frames. The latter is designed to be able to harden off without any of the oil being absorbed. Linseed oil putty on metal would never harden; certainly not within a reasonable time.

Lay a bed of fresh putty in the recess of the frame upon which the glass is pressed until it squeezes around the glass to cushion it against shock. Always press around the edges of a piece of glass—never in the centre. Secure the glass in a timber frame with headless tacks or springs. A couple each side is sufficient. The side of a chisel is the ideal hammer for this job, sliding it across the glass. On metal frames you will find small slots for wire clips and it is wise to use about two clips a side. You do not need to occupy all available holes.

With the glass secure, apply your finishing putty, angling it with a putty knife. This is not an easy job and it takes practice to get a good mitre at the corners. There are small glazing tools available which simplify the job for the beginner, but it is never easy the first time.

Make sure the putty does not come above the frame when viewed from inside. If it does, reduce the height of the putty with your knife. Allow your putty to harden for about a week before painting. When painting make sure the paint goes just on to the glass to seal the joint between glass and putty.

Loose glass in a leaded light

A true leaded light is quite a complicated structure. It is not easy to effect repairs as each piece of glass is actually set into an H-section of lead. Where panes rattle in the lead, buy a tube of lead adhesive of the type sold with imitation leaded light materials. This is a waterproof, transparent material, which is not visible when set.

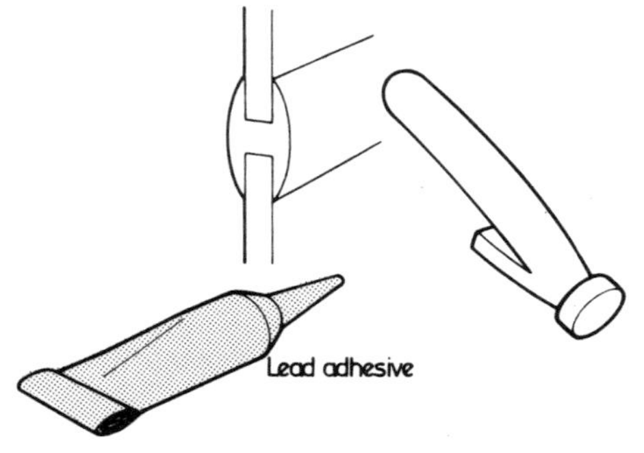

Squeeze a little into cracks in the window lead, then cut a clothes peg (as illustrated) to form a pressing tool. Press the lead gently back into place, where the adhesive will hold it.

If a pane is broken, after easing out the broken glass it will be necessary to cut and open three sides of the lead frame so that you can put in the new piece of glass. Then use the adhesive and your peg tool to get the lead back into place. Should the broken glass have been coloured, you can buy special glass colouring paints which are transparent and weather resistant.

Where a leaded light pane has completely deteriorated, put in a piece of plain glass, then build up the pattern using special lead strip sold for imitation leaded lights. This is either stuck in place with the special adhesive, or there is a new self-adhesive type ready to be stuck straight into place after removing a backing paper. The finished effect is quite good, but obviously if you can afford a replacement leaded light (custom built) this will still look better when closely examined.

The kits can be used to very good effect for changing the appearance of an existing set of windows. The simple diamond pattern will add character to the older house, and if you wish the upper lights could be coloured in a simple pattern.

Sticking doors

If a door does not close properly, assume that it did so at some time. Check first at the hinge side of the door. Tighten the screws as tight as they will go and very often this solves the problem. If this is not enough, and, if there us a reasonable gap at the hinge side, remove the door and deepen the hinge recesses slightly. This will widen the gap on the catch side by an equivalent amount.

Where there is no room to make this adjustment, then you may have to take some wood away at the catch edge. The tightness may be through a build-up of too many coats of paint. If you are not sure just where the door is sticking, slip a piece of carbon paper in the gap and shut the door. A mark will be left wherever the door catches and this is where you have to remove material.

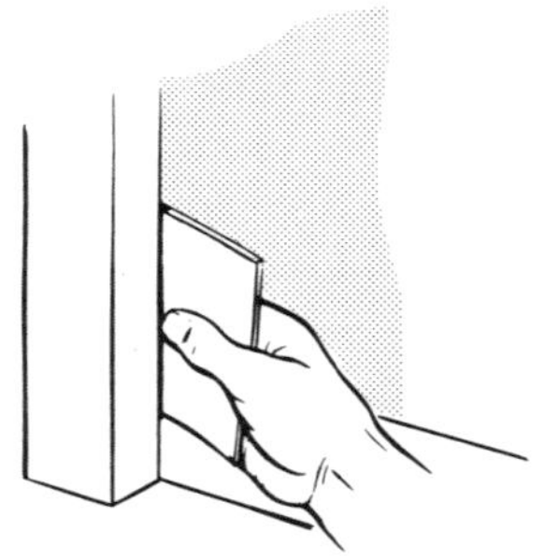

Very often the application of a drum sander is sufficient to ease the door. Failing this, use a shaping tool or, to take off a larger amount, a plane. If you have to plane, take the door off and secure it so that you can do the job properly.

The same advice applies where wood must be taken off the base of a door—perhaps because you have to put down underlay and carpet. Mark the door base where you wish to cut, and score through the paint with a knife. This helps prevent hard paint chipping away when you use a saw.

Use a fairly fine toothed hand saw working without applying too much pressure. The vertical stiles will cut easily, but the horizontal run of timber where you are cutting with the wood grain is never easy.

If only a small amount of wood needs to be removed, a plane would prove the easier tool to use. Work from each end when planing the vertical stiles, or you will split the wood when you come to the end.

Broken sash cords

Broken cords should never be ignored as a falling sash can be dangerous. As soon as one cord goes, it is advisable to replace them all. The cords are connected to weights which run in special pockets built into the window frames. It is these weights which counterbalance the weight of the window sash and make it easy to move.

To get at the cords, you remove the beading which is holding the sashes in place. These will be pinned, so prise them away with an old chisel. Now you will be able to pull the sash away. Cut the cord near the sash, and gently lower the weight down into the box. Remove the other sash in the same way, after taking out the centre beading which holds it in place.

You will see each box has a wood cover. Prise off the covers, then ease out the weights, lifting them clear of the boxes. Clean up the sashes by removing the staples holding the old sash cord in place, then put them aside. Now comes the tricky job of feeding new cord over the pulley wheels and down into the boxes. Tie a length of string to some poppet beads. Feed the beads over the wheels, then tie the new sash cord to the end of the string and feed it through. Remove the string and tie the new cord to the weight in the same way as the old cord was secured. Make sure that it cannot come loose! Now lower the weight back into its box.

Replace the box covers, oil the pulley wheels, and you are ready to fix the sash cords in place. The bottom sash will be using the inner pulleys, and the top sash the outer pulleys. For the top sash, allow the weights to rest on the bottom. Hold the sash in place at the top and mark where the pulley wheels come in relation to the sash. Hold the cord against the sash, and pull it out as you remove the sash. Fix the

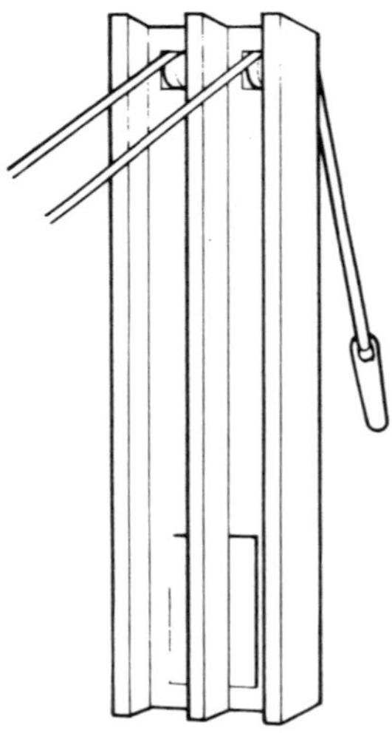

cord about 300 mm below the mark. Repeat for the other side. Trim off any surplus cord.

The lower sash needs the cords pulling down so that the weights rise to the top. Wedge the cords with the weights up to the top, then secure the cords to the top of the lower sash frame. The old marks will show you where to secure them. Trim off surplus cord. Test that the sash moves freely, then replace all the beadings.

The job sounds complicated, but it is one of those where you should note carefully how you dismantle the beadings and remove the cords. You can then merely work in reverse order when replacing everything.

Sticking curtain rails

If your home is fitted with old brass runners, it will pay you to strip them out and put in new plastic ones. These systems have improved tremendously in recent years.

To make the curtains run easier, remove the curtains, then apply a fine spray of aerosol lubricating and cleaning oil. Wipe off any surplus before putting curtains back.

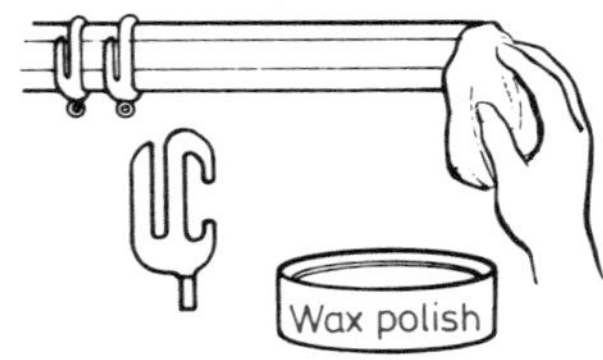

If you have more modern rails and these do not run freely, apply a little clear furniture polish to the runners and wipe off surplus. The same treatment can be used for curtain slides.

Ugly pipe runs

In older properties, pipes tend to run on the surface of walls, where they are an eyesore. In the larger kitchen where timber panelling would not be out of place, they could be lost in the gap between wall and new panelling fixed to timber battens a shade deeper than the pipes.

If you use this method, it is advisable to leave a slight gap top and bottom so that warm air can flow through during winter months. This, of course, applies where pipes are fixed on outer house walls. Interior partition walls will not get cold during winter.

Where it is not practicable to use panelling, the pipes can be boxed in, making a simple box of fibre board or hardboard

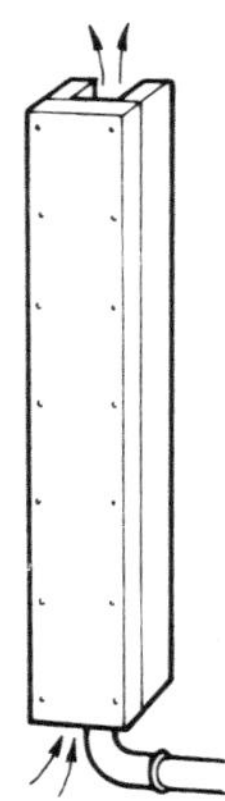

on a simple timber frame. Again, when working on outer walls, be sure to leave an air gap top and bottom. If the pipes are isolated from the room, they could freeze.

Hollow wall fixing

Modern methods of partitioning may be easy to build, but they can be tricky to fix things on to because they have a hollow core. To fix heavy cabinets you need to find the vertical timber studding in the wall and use this for anchor points. A horizontal batten fixed to the studding can be used to rest a cabinet on, then you only need screws to hold the unit to the wall.

To make these fixings you need special hollow fixing anchors. These come in a number of types, but the basic principle

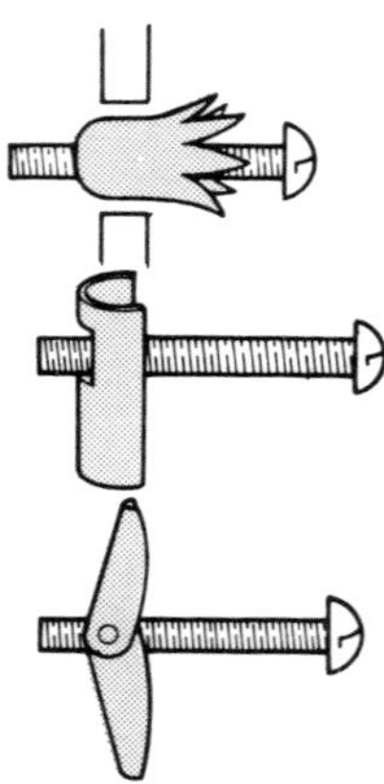

is the same. Part of the fixing is fed into the cavity of the partition, where it is anchored, forming a good grip when the screw is tightened. Most ordinary wall plugs are not suitable as they can get little grip on the partition, and will probably disappear into the cavity.

Similar cavity fixings will have to be employed when securing items like new wall sockets. If you are about to put up new partitioning, it would pay you to knock pieces of timber into the cavity of the partition at points likely to be used for fixing. The timber will give you a far stronger anchorage than any fixing device.

Resurfacing laminates

Where you encounter laminate worktops or table tops which you would like to replace, wherever possible leave the old laminate in place and put a new one over the top. Score the old laminate thoroughly with a coarse abrasive pad to give a good key for the next sheet, then apply adhesive to both surfaces as you would for any contact fixing. Allow the surfaces to become touch-dry, then bring the two surfaces together.

Door slamming

In modern homes particularly, lightweight flush doors tend to swing open and slam shut very easily. This is accentuated during fine weather when doors are left open and winds are quite strong—with the potential danger to the smaller members of the family and the danger of glass doors being damaged.

Small but efficient door closers are available which will effectively control movement of the door and prevent it swinging free. These modern closers are small and unobtrusive.

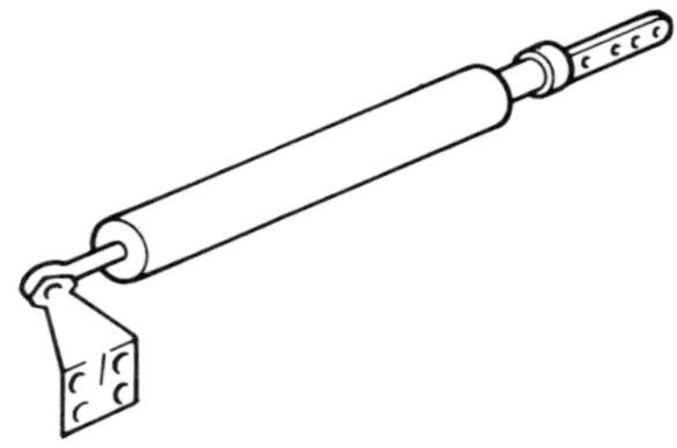

To stop a door banging when it shuts, fit a small rubber dome of silencer to the door frame so that the door hits the rubber first. If there is little clearance available, you may have to trim the dome down. Where there is the minimum of room use a small strip of foam rubber draught excluder as a buffer.

Damaged plaster mouldings

In some older properties, ornate mouldings are used both as cornices and as ceiling decoration. If pieces have become damaged, small areas can be built up with cellulose filler, then when set rubbed down with glasspaper and rasp to match the surrounding area.

Where a shaped cornice is involved, fill the damaged area with cellulose filler proud of the surface, then make up a simple template cut from sheet metal. Pull the template over the filler so that it scrapes away the surplus material until the repair matches the surrounding moulding.

If the damaged area is intricate—i.e. flowers or leaves—you can buy a special rubber moulding material which can be melted then used to make a female mould

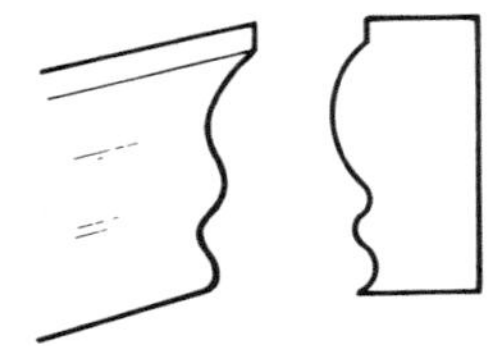

from an existing piece of decoration. When set, the mould can be pulled away, then the mould filled with casting powder mixed to a creamy consistency with water. This will reproduce a perfect replica of the decoration and it can then be cut into the damaged area and stuck in place. Very accurate repairs can be made in this way.

Post pulling from the wall

Very often the weight of a gate will pull the post away from a supporting wall. This is usually because the builder merely used a wedge of wood as a wall plug into which the securing screw or screws were driven. When the wood shrinks or rots, the post comes away.

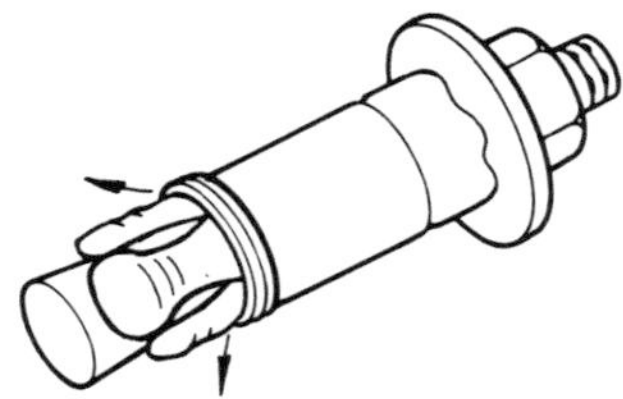

Buy an anchor bolt long enough to pass through the post and at least 40 mm (1½ in) into the wall. You may have to buy a star drill to make a hole in the wall to take the bolt, as the bolt will be bigger than the average large masonry drill. The bolt is inserted into the wall then, as the unit is tightened, a cone in the bolt is pulled up, spreading the bolt sections and jamming it firmly in the wall. The post will then have a very firm anchorage point. In normal circumstances, two such bolts are all that is needed.

Noise through a window

Even double glazing will not completely cut out noise from outside, as the panes are too close together. To cut down noise you need to add another pane of glass at least 75 mm (3 in) away from the existing one. This new glass should be of different weight to ensure that the pane does not vibrate in sympathy with the existing one.

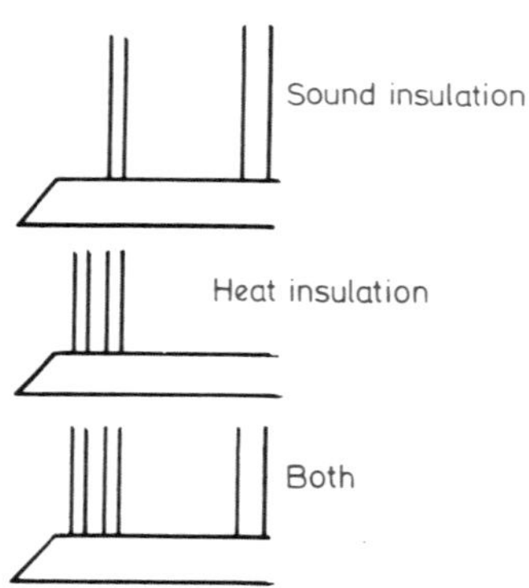

Make sure there are no gaps around the frame and, of course, opening a window immediately cancels out the effect of insulation.

Chapter 10
Seventy repair tips

In tackling the many repair jobs around your home, it is possible to waste valuable materials and time through quite small mistakes. The following tips are designed to make you wise to some of the pitfalls and positive wrinkles. They are based on many years of experience. The tips are subdivided to make reference easier.

Timber and boards

If you have to nail into hardwood, such as is used for beadings, drill fine holes through the wood to take the nails. This will greatly reduce the risk of splitting. Do not nail too near edges, and try to avoid lining nails along wood grain. A staggered row will help prevent splitting. When using screws a similar rule applies. You should use slightly larger start holes for hardwood than for soft woods to avoid splitting. Never overtighten screws—especially when using brass or alloy ones. You can easily turn the heads off when a dense timber cannot give.

Where timber used for fence boards has warped badly, remove each board and nail a piece of scrap wood on each end to act as a handle. Soak the board until saturated with water, then move it over a garden fire, forcing a twist into it, counter to the direction of the warp. The steam produced will make the board pliable and you will be able to get the board straight. Weight the board until quite dry, then replace in the fence.

Where a number of boards are involved, the steam generated by a steam wallpaper stripping machine will make the job easier. Wear leather gloves to avoid scalding.

Dowelled joints are ideal for making strong joins in timber, and they are particularly good for strengthening joints in veneered chipboards. There are a number of dowelling jigs on the market which simplify accurate alignment.

You can make your own dowels from lengths of dowel rod, and a simple way to reduce the size of a dowel is to drill a suitably sized hole in a piece of mild steel sheet. Anchor the sheet, then tap the dowel

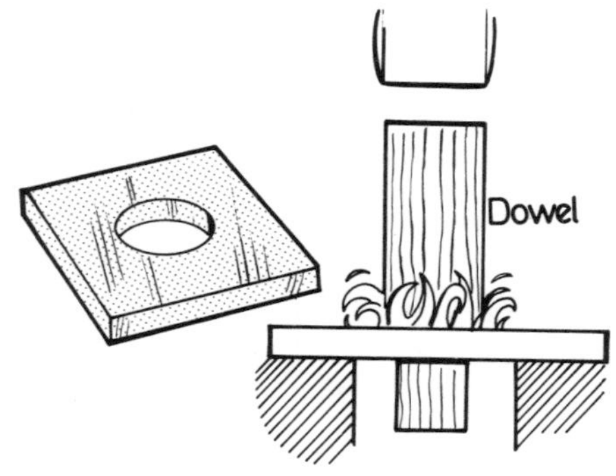

through the hole using a wood or rubber mallet. To reduce from large to quite small, use a number of holes and work down from one to the other until the required size is obtained.

It is possible to shape plywood by cutting through the laminates to a set depth. This is best done with a power saw where the depth of cut can be accurately set on the depth gauge. The amount of bend will be governed by the spacing of the cuts, and it is well worthwhile experimenting with scrap material before moving on to an actual job.

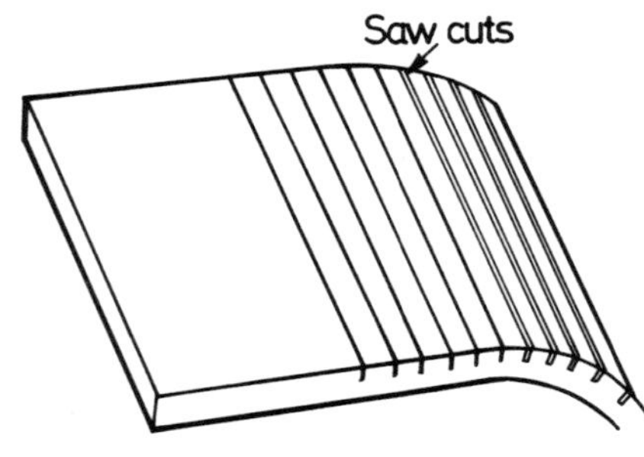

It is also important that the cuts made are truly parallel with each other so that your curve is true. A saw bench, where the wood is run over the saw blade, and where an accurate fence guide can be used, will produce the best work.

When shaping or cutting sections of timber, there is always the danger of splitting or breaking. You can reduce the risk by clamping up your piece alongside one or two pieces of scrap timber, then working all together. In this way, the good material is protected and held firm. The same rule applies when planing or shaping across end grain where there is a real danger of splitting an edge. Where a piece of wood has to be shaped along its length, if possible leave a spare area of wood at each end by which the work can be held. Then cut this off when shaping is complete.

Making a timber joint by drilling into end grain may be a simple way of putting pieces together, but it does not give much strength. You can produce a far better job by inserting a dowel, positioned so that

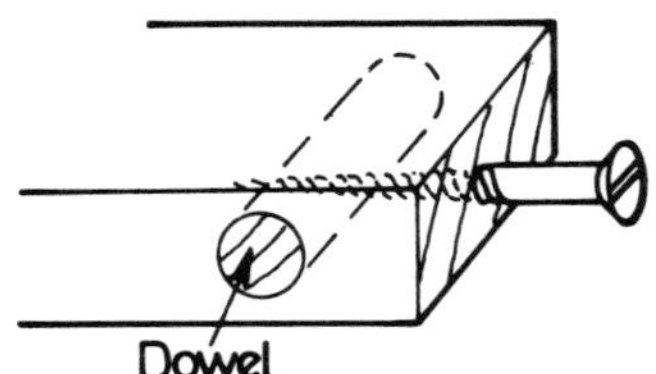

when you screw into the end grain, the screw will be anchored in the dowel. A start-hole in the dowel will ensure the screw enters properly without splitting the wood. Don't rely only on screws. Apply a wood glue to the meeting pieces before screwing-up — applying extra to the end grain to allow for absorption.

Where the hole in a screwed joint has become enlarged — perhaps through movement — remove the screw, then enlarge the hole to take a ribbed plastic wall plug, tapping it in flush with the wood. Now you can use the same size screw as previously, but it will anchor far better in the plug. If the plug is of the expanding type, make sure it expands into the widest section of the timber — not across the narrowest dimension. With large holes — such as in fencing — it is possible to push one wall plug into another to get a good grip.

With timber prices so high these days, quality is sometimes questionable. For carcase repair work, the occasional knot — or even missing knot — may cause little trouble. But where timber is to be used decoratively, and particularly where it will get warm, avoid all but really sound knots. They may work loose after you have decorated the timber. Patent knotting will seal a knot so that no resin is exuded after painting.

An exception to the rule is where timber is to be used for decorative interior panelling. Here, knots can look attractive, and polyurethane wood seal can be used to anchor them in place.

For most timber repair jobs where new timber is to be inserted, plan to make your insert over-size so that it stands proud of the timber surface. When the adhesive is hard, use a shaping tool or rasp to rough shape the wood to the surrounding area, then finish off with a sander, working only with the wood grain, until the whole area is smooth. Where there are slight gaps, work a fine surface filler into them, allow to set and finally sand smooth. Always prime bare wood before redecorating. If fine nails were used to hold the new wood, punch them below the wood surface, fill the holes and smooth before priming.

Where timber is to be used indoors, bring it inside a week or two before use. This applies particularly during the wet winter months where the moisture content between outdoors and in a centrally heated home may be very considerable. Leaving it indoors will allow the timber to adjust its content while it can still move freely. To prevent hardboard buckling indoors, sprinkle the back of sheets with water and store back to back for a few days before using. This will allow the board to adapt to its surroundings.

Glass

Wherever you have to handle glass, it pays to wear a pair of leather gardening gloves as edges can be very sharp.If glass has to be handled quite a bit, use the edge of a carborundum stone to rub down and remove sharpness. Even a few minute's work will make the glass safe to handle. Where plate glass is to be used for replacement sliding doors perhaps to a cupboard, it is worth paying the extra at the glaziers to have the edges ground to shape. This will ensure that the doors run smoothly. Carry large pieces of glass vertically, protected by paper. Carrying it flat may cause it to break merely through its own weight.

Do not store old glass against the day when it can be used again. For some reason it ages and becomes very hard to cut accurately. Wherever possible buy fresh glass as you need it. Unless you have considerable experience, choose a wheel glass cutter — not a diamond-tipped cutter. The diamond works very well in the hands of an expert. Good wheel cutters are provided with extra wheels, so move the cutter on as a wheel becomes dulled. You should hear the cutter whispering over the glass if it is cutting well.

Glazed panels in doors — and particularly exterior doors — always present an accident hazard. A door may slam violently in the wind, or a person may fall against it. Wherever there is a risk it will pay to fit a toughened glass. You can now buy a special laminated glass which has a tough plastic film sandwiched between two pieces of glass. This makes it tremendously tough, and while it will craze, it will not break or form dangerous splinters. It costs more than standard glass, but the investment is worth the extra.

Wherever an awkward shaped piece of glass has to be replaced, don't rely on measurements alone. Make an accurate template from stiff brown paper or thin card — allowing about 3 mm all round so that putty can cushion the glass in its frame. Where such a piece was leaded, a good imitation leaded light can be made using self-adhesive lead strip and special glass stains. You need to make a patterned template, then lay the glass on this while the lead is added. Use coloured stains on the inside. A slightly irregular application of glass stain colours will look more like real stained glass.

There is no satisfactory way of repairing cracked glass, but the crack can be sealed by applying a special waterproof transparent adhesive tape. It is best to apply this as soon as possible, before dirt has time to get into the cracks. Look upon the seal as a temporary repair only.

Where patterned glass is used in exterior doors or windows, insert new glass with the pattern side in so that the smoothest face can be sealed against the weather. This is particularly important where glass is held in place by a timber beading, for it is vital that no rain can get down behind the beading. Rain entering at this point is one of the commonest causes of door frame rot. Another advantage of having the pattern side in is that there is nothing on the outside to collect dirt and grime, and window cleaning will be easier.

Use plenty of bedding putty with patterned glass so that all gaps are adequately sealed between frame and glass.

To temporarily obscure glass, whiting or window cleaning liquid left to dry on the window will do. But where you wish to obscure the glass to give permanent privacy, there are self-adhesive plastic sheets available in a number of decorative patterns. Clean the glass thoroughly, strip off just a little of the backing paper, position the sheet, then pull away the rest of the backing paper. Press edges well down to prevent moisture getting under and lifting the sheet.

If you prefer to do the job with patterned glass, a good variety is available from most glaziers.

If you wish to drill a hole in glass, use a special glass drill either in a wheel brace, or in a power tool of the type which has a good speed reducer. High speed is a distinct disadvantage. A small piece of transparent adhesive tape will help you position the tip of the drill, and it pays to make a little 'well' around the mark with Plasticine, into which a little oil or turps can be poured to act as a lubricant. As the drill tip breaks through, turn the glass over and finish off from the other side to avoid splintering the edges of the hole as the drill breaks through. Apply the very minimum of pressure at all times and don't try to rush the job.

This is really a non-tip, but it is one that crops up very regularly. There is no easy or cheap way to re-silver mirror glass. Once the mirror deteriorates, it is wise to replace it, or take it to a glaziers for re-silvering. The materials needed are not easy to obtain and some are dangerous to handle. Producing a good mirror finish is still a job for the experts!

When using mirror clips to hold a mirror to a wall, it is always wise to use soft washers between wall and mirror back. This is to absorb any minor irregularities in wall surface which could otherwise impose a severe strain on the mirror. Never overtighten holding screws — in fact err on the loose side for safety.

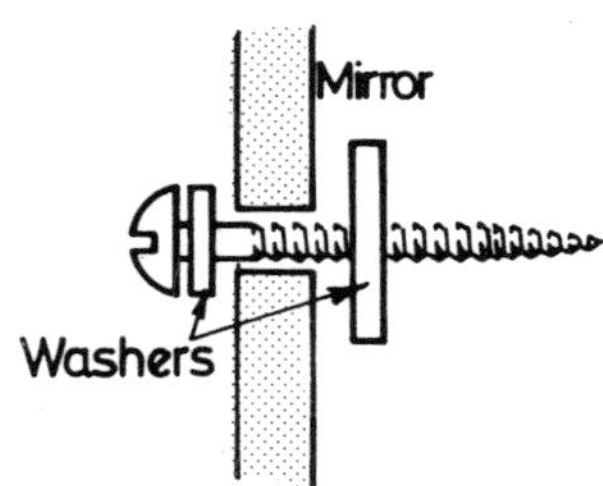

Lightweight mirrors or mirror tiles can be held by special double-sided adhesive pads, but they must always be applied to clean, dry, grease-free surfaces. You can stick on to tile, plaster or well adhering paint. You cannot stick to wallpaper or vinyl wallcoverings.

Brick

Unless you are experienced at using a bricklaying trowel, cut a brick by using a bolster and club hammer. Place the brick on a bed of sand to absorb the impact, then tap a line with bolster and hammer, leaving a clear vee nick in the brick. When there is a clear mark, increase the impact and give one sharp blow along the line. The brick should break clean. The same technique can be used for shaping or cleaning up. The rough face of a brick can be smoothed with an abrasive cutting wheel used in a power tool, but take great care. Wear protective gloves — and safety specs.

Cleaning decorative brickwork is not easy, as soaps and detergents leave stains. A scrubbing brush and clean water are best, with a wire brush used for obstinate marks. Where you encounter mortar stains, perhaps through careless bricklaying, the mortar marks can be removed by using a special chemical cleaner used by builders for cleaning their tools. It dissolves cement mortar without affecting the bricks. Ask at your largest builders merchants for details.

Drilling holes in brick is best done with a special masonry drill. This should be of a size to match the wall plugs and screws you plan to use. The masonry drill can be used in a hand wheel brace, but it is easier to use if mounted in the chuck of a power drill. Use the lowest speed you can. Ease the drill from the wall occasionally to clear the brick dust and to allow the tip to cool. Always drill under applied pressure, and never let the tip just skate over the surface.

Where larger holes are needed — such as when fixing a post to a wall with anchor bolts — use a special star drill, which is made in sizes to match bolts. This is tapped smartly with a hammer, and slowly rotated as the drill bites.

Special long drills and extension drills are available where extra deep holes are required.

Brick and briquette fireplaces can discolour with age, and cleaning is not easy. Use the technique already mentioned for brick cleaning, plus the addition of a rub with a piece of matching brick. When clean, colour can often be restored by using special brick stains, available in a limited range of colours. These restore the brick colours without affecting the surface. It is never wise to use coloured seals as these block the pores of the brick and add an unnatural sheen.

If an open fire is used, a stainless steel surround fitted in the fireplace opening is a good investment. It will prevent sooting up of brickwork.

Where exterior bricks are over-porous, they can be sealed with a silicone water repellent which prevents the ingress of moisture while still allowing the brickwork to 'breathe'. It should be applied liberally so it flows over the surface — but keep it off woodwork and window glass. It is very hard to remove from such surfaces.

Cement/Concrete

It is always wise to buy fresh cement as you need it, for it is not an easy material to store. If you must store it for a while, place the opened bag in a tough polythene bag or sack and seal the top. Store the pack in the dry, and don't rest it on a floor likely to get wet. For small repair jobs buy a small pack of ready-mix, and don't open any more than you can use. Cover sand and aggregates, especially during wet weather, as the moisture content can change dramatically. It is not possible to use cement which has hardened in the bag. Don't be tempted to powder it down and use it. Throw it out.

Cement works best with the minimum of moisture, so always err on the dry side when mixing concrete. Apart from strength, a sloppy mix is likely to stain surrounding areas; it will be hard to place and it won't hold its shape. So that a dry mix retains its strength while setting, damp the surfaces to which it is to be applied. This applies also to mortar, for the joints should be damped with a paint brush and water so that moisture is not drawn from the mortar mix.

There are times when plain concrete can look rather stark, and it is now possible to stain concrete, toning it down to match other surfaces or applying a decorative colour. Applications include staining concrete spurs holding fencing so the spurs are less conspicuous, and painting plain paths and patios to give the appearance of crazy paving. Stains are permanent and need no protective coating.

Where paths and patios are used during icy weather, it is wise to consider making them non-slip. This can be done during building by ridging the concrete just before it sets, or by including an aggregate and brushing away the top cement before it sets to expose stones. Paving slabs can be made with a layer of stones as a top dressing, or fine stones can be embedded into concrete before it sets. Don't go to the other extreme and make the surface a danger to small children if they fall!

A reasonable non-slip surface can be produced by adding silver sand to a good quality exterior grade emulsion paint. It needs regular stirring to keep the sand suspended, and it must be applied to clean surfaces.

Concrete will lose strength if it dries too rapidly after laying. The damper it can be kept, the better. Old sacking damped with water is ideal during warm weather, or failing that use polythene sheeting. Rain will rarely affect drying concrete. In fact it will prolong the curing period. Don't lay concrete during periods of frost. Wait until the weather improves.

It is essential to clean off all tools used for concrete work — particularly those you may have hired, such as a concrete mixer. Most can be washed off with water, but obstinate layers can be removed while 'green' (not yet hardened) with a coarse wire brush. Really hard concrete should be dissolved with a special chemical cleaner available from builders merchants.

Clean up splashes on paths and walls as they occur. Don't wait until the concrete hardens. The chemical referred to will remove stains from brick without affecting the brickwork.

Make sure you get the right sand for the job in hand. Sharp sand, which is clean but gritty, is fine for paths and drives. But for mortar mixes choose a soft sand which gives a soft, buttery mix — but which stains the hands. When ordering, clearly specify the purpose for which the sand is going to be used.

When filling a childrens' sand pit, always choose a sharp sand — never a soft builders sand. As already mentioned, the soft sand will stain. Put a cover over your sand pit to keep off animals and to prevent debris blowing in.

Where concrete tends to flake or pull away from an under-layer of concrete, use a pva adhesive to bond them together. The adhesive can be used as an additive to the water in the actual mix, and also it can be brush-applied to the surface to be covered just before the new material is laid. In this way, concrete can be feathered down to nothing and still not flake.

The pva can also be used to coat dusting concrete. Brush the surface clean, apply a layer of pva with a brush, and it will effectively seal the surface.

Making fixings to concrete can be tackled in the same way as for brick, using a masonry drill or star drill. When plugging, make sure the plugs are suitable for outdoor use. Dense concrete with a sharp aggregate is very hard to drill, and it may be necessary

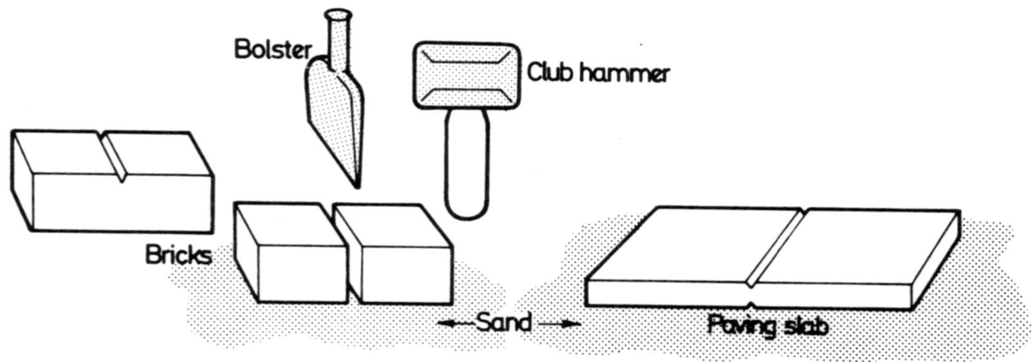

to use a hammer and jumping tool to break stones. A good alternative is to use a power tool with hammer action — combining the best of drilling and hammering. Where items like sheds and greenhouses have to be secured to concrete, always choose an expanding type anchor rather than a normal plug. They give far better anchorage.

Cutting slabs calls for practice, so try out your technique on broken pieces before cutting good slabs.

Lay the slab on a bed of sand to cushion the impact, then tap a line on the slab using bolster and club hammer until a clear vee nick is formed. Turn the slab over and repeat the operation. Now place the bolster on the slab, in the cut, and tap smartly. The slab should break clean along the mark. When you are experienced, you should be able to split a slab without turning it over.

Taking off narrow strips is quite hard, and it calls for care in making the initial vee nick. It may be safer to nibble the waste away with two or three cuts with the bolster, rather than trying to remove the strip in one piece.

Electrics

While an excellent book on electrics exists in this series — *Home Electrics* — a few tips on electrical repairs will not be amiss here.

While the rigid plastic used for plugs and sockets can usually be repaired with an epoxy resin adhesive, it is very good practice to remove and replace all damaged fittings. Never get into the habit of making 'temporary' repairs with adhesive tape, whether insulating or not. If plugs or connectors are likely to get knocked about, choose rubber replacements which are unbreakable. Where lampholders are subject to considerable heat — as in enclosed shades — use brass lampholders rather than plastic. Make sure the flex used is also heat-resistant.

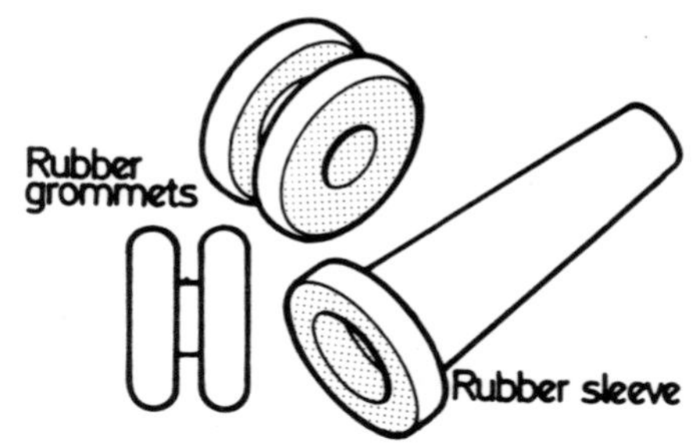

Wherever flex passes through metal or thin section plastic, be sure to fit a rubber grommet. This ensures that the flex cannot be damaged by sharp edges constantly rubbing. Where flex is constantly on the move — as with an electric iron flex — fit a rubber sleeve close to the iron so that it takes the brunt of any wear. Replace it when it becomes worn. Whenever flex shows sign of fatigue, replace it before any real damage is done. Replace the whole length. Don't connect in a new piece of flex.

If a socket is loose on the wall, and the screws fail to tighten, the problem may be that the wall is hollow. Switch off the electricity supply; remove the socket from the wall and check. If the wall is solid, new wall plugs may be all that is necessary. If you encounter a hollow wall, you need special cavity wall anchors designed to grip on the inside of the partition. These take various forms, from those operated by a gravity toggle, to a type which splays out as tightened. Don't tighten holding screws more than is necessary or you may damage the partition.

Where a surface-mounted switch is loose, you will need to get at the base plate. Disconnect the power, remove the switch cover and try to tighten the two holding screws in the base plate. They may just have worked loose. If they won't tighten, release the wires to the switch, remove the screws and pull the plate away — having noted which wires go where. You may need to put in new wall plugs before replacing the plate. If the plate is damaged, replace the switch.

If a flush mounted switch is loose, even with the two screws tight, it is likely that the box housed in the wall is loose. Switch off the power, remove the cover and ease it and the connected wires away from the wall. Check to see if the screws holding the box are tight. If not, tighten. If they will not tighten, you must disconnect the wiring taking note of which wire goes where. Take out the box; re-plug the wall and replace, making sure none of the wiring is trapped by the box. Re-wire the switch.

Where a ceiling rose is loose, switch off the power, remove the cover by unscrewing, to expose the pattress (that section of the rose connected to the ceiling). Check whether the retaining screws have worked loose. If they will not tighten it may be that the screws were merely driven into the ceiling plaster — which is not adequate for mounting. Ideally you need to get into the space above the fitting by lifting a floorboard, then place a piece of wood between the ceiling joists so that the screws can be driven into this wood through the plaster. If this is not possible, you may be able to use cavity fixings as mentioned for hollow walls.

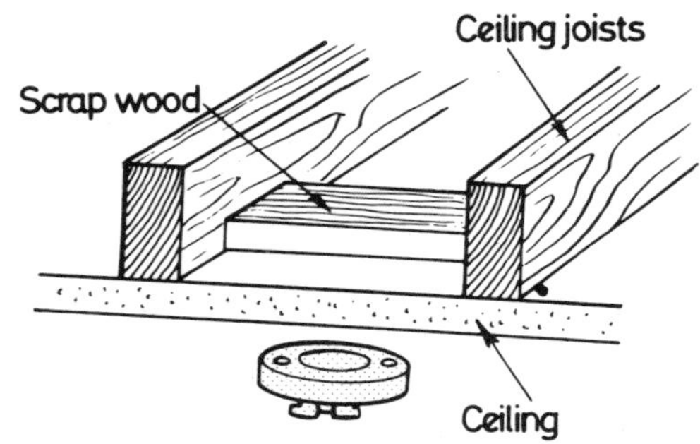

If outside wiring to sheds or garages does not work, it is essential to check it very carefully. Disconnect the cable from the mains supply then check the cable run. It must either be carried overhead, supported by a steel cable capable of supporting it, or it must be connected by means of a special underground cable. On no account can power be carried by a cable draped along a fence or laid on earth. If in any doubt, check with our book on ***HOME ELECTRICS.***

If flex must be joined, be sure to use proper flex connectors so that a good screwed joint is produced. Wherever wires are to branch off, use a connector box with screwed terminals. Do not accept taped joints. Where flex is to be used out of doors, and it needs to be extended, use the correct three terminal male and female connectors, with the female always on the live end of the extension. Another safe way of extending is to use an extension cable reel. Taped joints are never acceptable for outdoor extensions.

Where you find flex is run under carpets or rugs, remove it and find a safer route. This is the most common cause of flex failure leading to a short circuit and perhaps a fire. Flex is not designed to be constantly trodden on. Pin the flex to the skirting board with insulated staples, or tuck under the skirting board if there is a gap. Ideally fit new socket outlets so that flex does not need to be run to standard and table lamps. New socket outlets must be correctly wired to cable — never to flex.

In an older property, where you encounter rubber-sheathed cables where the sheath is hardening, it is a clear indication that the property is ready for re-wiring. Don't be tempted to patch it up (see the book on *Home Electrics*). Perished cables are a real danger and they greatly add to the risk of fire.

Plumbing

There is now a good book on *Home Plumbing* in the d-i-y series, so only a few minor repairs are mentioned here.

If the overflow in the loft is dripping water, suspect the ball valve in the cold water storage tank. You may need a new valve seating, or the ball may have failed. As an emergency repair for a punctured ball float, empty out the water, then slip a polythene bag over the ball and secure with an elastic band. Modern ball floats made of plastic have a far better chance of survival — and they will not corrode. Plastic valves are also available which make far less noise than older patterns.

If a tap continues to drip after fitting a new washer, the valve seating may be damaged. It is possible to grind a new flat surface on the valve, but if you are unable to do this, buy a new plastic valve seating designed to be pushed on top of the old one. This will give the tap a new lease of life. A nylon jumper unit is also available to go with the new seating.

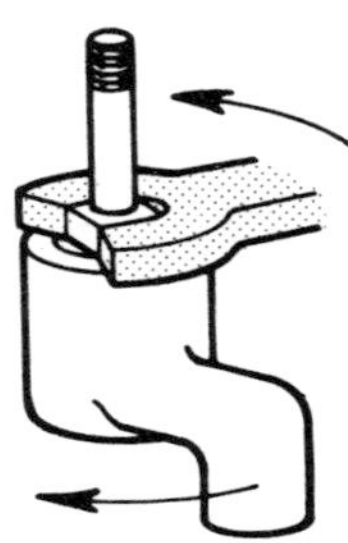

A damaged water pipe can be repaired with a modern resin-hardener paste, but it needs to be reinforced by glass fibre tape. The paste on its own has not sufficient strength. Apply paste, wind on a turn of bandage and apply a further layer of paste, then another wind of bandage. An extremely strong repair can be made in this way. After a freezing spell, check exposed compression joints, as pressure may have forced them loose.

Take great care when loosening or tightening nuts on basins, for it is very easy to crack the basin. The secret is to apply an equal force to, for example, a tap as to the nut you are trying to undo, thus cancelling out any strain on the basin itself. If you must try to tap any part loose, use a rubber faced hammer which will not cause any damage. Wherever nuts will not move, apply easing oil, then give the oil chance to work. This often works where force fails.

If you encounter water hammer — a severe knocking in pipes when a cistern is filling — suspect the ball valve vibrating up and down as the valve starts to close. You can buy a special paddle designed to damp the movement which clips to the ball arm. Or, make a damper from a plastic beaker suspended from the ball arm by wire, and completely submerged in the water.

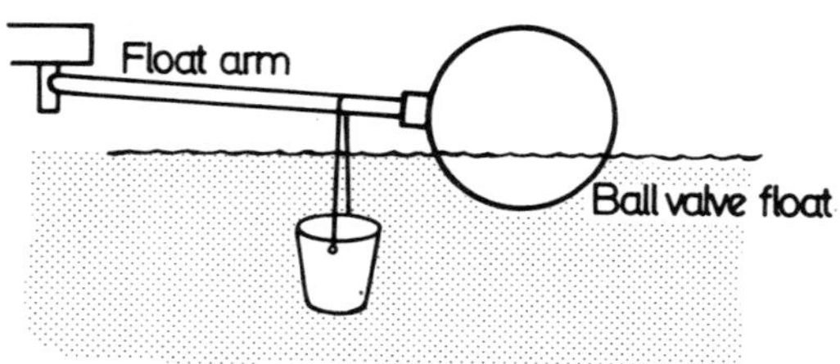

Another cause of hammer is the jumper of the tap washer moving up and down. A captive jumper will often cure this trouble.

Gaps around baths and basins are a problem, as the gap can vary in size according to movement. So a flexible seal of some kind is necessary. A silicone rubber sealant applied to clean, dry surfaces will give a good flexible seal — but it takes practice to get a really smooth finish. If you are applying new tiles, you can buy quadrant tile sets designed to hide the gap and blend with your tiling. This joint is not flexible, so the quadrant must extend far enough over the bath or basin to ensure that water drains off.

Where you encounter leaking pipe joints which will not respond to tightening, there is a tape available (called ptfe tape) which will ensure a good seal. It is easier and less messy to use than the old boss white paste. The joint is opened, tape wound around the thread, then the joint re-made. Where a compression joint will not tighten, suspect the cone or the olive, which is designed to make a seal without undue pressure. If damaged or deformed, replace it. Capillary joints which leak must be heated to separate, then the joint re-made. The joint cannot be patched from the outside.

If the joint between the lavatory pan and the waste pipe is leaking, empty the pan as far as possible and allow the joint time to dry. Now dig out any crumbling filling from the joint, then fill with glazing cord or tape. This is a mastic-like material applied to cord or bandage, and when tamped well home, it will give a good watertight joint. Give a final smooth with your finger. The surface will become touch-dry, but the joint will remain flexible.

A chip in a basin is not easy to disguise, but it can be built up using a liquid porcelain paint. This should be applied one coat at a time, then left to harden before the next layer is applied. Repeat the process until the paint is flush with the surrounding material. If done well, the repair will be hard to spot. For repairs out of sight, a ceramic putty is ideal. This comes as two parts which, as required are mixed together, after which hardening is by chemical action. Once set, the putty can be painted to match the unit.

Ideally a central heating system should contain an inhibitor liquid to prevent corrosion of the formation of sludge. If you find a pinhole in a radiator with water weeping out, buy a radiator sealing liquid and feed it into the sealed system by way of the small expansion tank in the loft. This will seal off minor leaks. Systems not containing an inhibitor are best drained off, re-filled with clean water, then an inhibitor added via the small expansion tank.

Plastics

Thermosetting plastics — those unaffected by heating — can usually be repaired using an epoxy resin adhesive or the cyanoacrylate type adhesive. As already mentioned, don't make a habit of mending broken electrical appliances; replace them. Assemble broken pieces dry first to ensure where they fit, before coating with adhesive. A quick-setting epoxy will enable you to hold the repair. It will harden in five minutes. A cyanoacrylate sets in about ten seconds! Don't get it on your fingers!

Polythenes cannot be bonded with adhesives. They seem to grip while wet, but once dry, drop away. Polythene can be welded by using a warm soldering iron over a piece of aluminium foil. Or sheet polythene can be welded using a special welding wheel — rather like a soldering iron with a wheel at the end — or by using the edge of a warm domestic iron applied over a piece of foil. Never apply the iron direct to the polythene. It may melt on the sole plate of the iron and be very hard to remove! Polythene can be held temporarily by self-adhesive plastic tape.

Polystyrene can be repaired with a special polystyrene adhesive of the type used for assembling plastic toy kits. The adhesive contains a solvent which softens the polystyrene, so make sure you do not spill it on decorative surfaces. This adhesive is not designed for expanded polystyrene.

Expanded polystyrene can be stuck with one of the adhesives sold for fixing ceiling tiles or holding wall veneer. It should never be used with an adhesive containing powerful solvents, as the solvent destroys the structure of the foam. For a good waterproof joint between expanded polystyrene and other materials, use a black exterior grade rubber adhesive. The solvent is mild enough not to damage the foam.

Synthetic rubbers such as used for pulley belts and drive belts can be very rapidly stuck using cyanoacrylate adhesive. Providing the surfaces meet well, bonding time is measured in seconds, though full strength may take an hour or so. Bear in mind that a belt which shows signs of deterioration is best replaced as soon as possible. The adhesive may well keep the appliance in use until a new belt can be obtained.

Plastic trims where the material is flexible are best secured with a rubber based adhesive. Items such as car trims where the weather is an enemy can be stuck in place with a silicone rubber sealing compound, which also acts as a very effective adhesive. Surfaces to be stuck must of course be clean, free from dust and loose rust — and they must be dry.

Scratches on acrylic plastic surfaces — such as on an acrylic bath — can be polished out using metal polish wadding. It takes time, and care should be taken to blend in the area with its surrounding plastic. Acrylics are easily scratched, so avoid scouring powders. Keep paint strippers and hot cigarettes away too!

Most thermoplastics can be handled easier when warmed. If shaping is possible, the plastic needs to be heated. Use hot water for mild warming, or a hair dryer for greater heat. The hair dryer, for example, is ideal for softening a vinyl floor tile which has lifted. When warmed, it will go down on to new adhesive much more readily. Thermosetting plastics do not respond to warming.

Most plastics can be drilled. Hard materials can be drilled at speed, but the plastics which soften with heat are best hand drilled at the lowest possible speed. Otherwise you can soften the plastic enough for it to melt on to the twist drill.

Plastic laminates can be cut with a knife fitted with a special laminate cutting blade. The surface of the laminate is scored, then the sheet bent *up* (not down) with the pattern side up. It can also be cut with a fine tooth saw, and the edges smoothed with a cabinet scraper, a fine rasp or very fine glasspaper. It can be drilled with normal twist drills, and stuck in place with rubber-based adhesive.

Floorcoverings

If a small area of carpet is damaged—perhaps by a burn – cut out a square just taking in the damaged area and insert a matching square. It can be held in place with a small square of hessian soaked with latex adhesive, or by using a square of carpet binding tape. If any tufts stand proud, press down, then trim lightly with scissors.

Where carpet is fraying at the edges, turn back the edge and secure with latex carpet adhesive or with carpet tape. Trim off any loose strands. To prevent fraying of other sections, coat the back of the carpet for a width of about 50 mm to bind all the threads together. This helps particularly with some of the cheaper grade carpets where fraying starts as soon as the carpet is cut to size.

Where carpet or vinyl is lifting at doorways, it pays to buy an edging strip to hold it down. These are available in various types, to secure either one edge of carpet; two edges, or an edge of carpet one side and vinyl the other. The strip is designed to be screwed in place, and if correctly fitted it will offer no obstruction to a door.

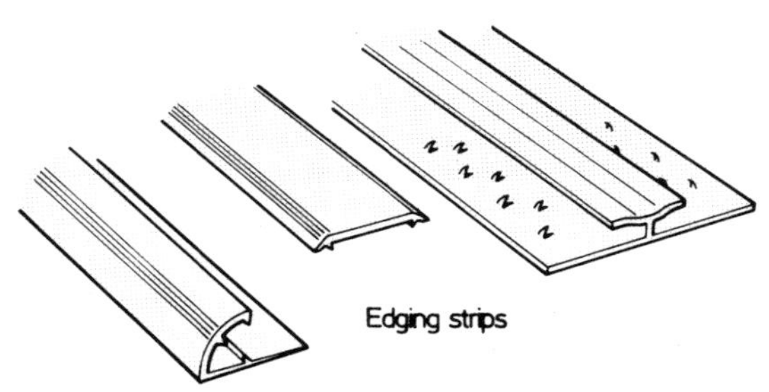
Edging strips

Where a vinyl floorcovering has been scuffed by shoe marks, rub the area with a pad of fine wire wool lubricated with turps. This will remove the marks without damaging the floor. Ideally, areas like parquet and decorative vinyl should be protected by runners – or outdoor shoes should be barred from the house!

Where a rug tends to creep, or where a runner slides, secure it with small squares of self-adhesive Velcro tape. This has fine hooks and loops which hold firmly, but which can very easily be separated when necessary.

Alternatively, use carpet press studs for runners where it does not matter if you screw into the floor. If it does matter, use rubberised netting under the runner. This very effectively anchors a carpet.

Index

Further helpful reading

Beginner's Guides are pocket-sized but contain an enormous amount of information of interest to DIY enthusiasts, from novices to old hands who insist they are well past the 'beginner' stage!

For example, **Beginner's Guide to Domestic Plumbing** gives clear, concise coverage, with detailed illustrations, of all that the householder needs to know about domestic plumbing design and materials, the techniques of hot and cold water supply, sanitary installations and drainage. For those easily baffled by electrics, **Beginner's Guide to Electric Wiring** is an easily readable yet authoritative guide requiring no previous technical knowledge. It covers the planning and installation of wiring, accessories and fittings in the home and workshop – always with the emphasis on safety and conformity with the Wiring Regulations. If you want to produce well-finished woodwork, **Beginner's Guide to Woodworking** is an introduction to this satisfying craft that will increase both theoretical knowledge and practical skill. It describes clearly the tools and methods used by professional carpenters and joiners, so that the reader can put into practice their basic techniques.

For the more ambitious do-it-yourselfer, **Beginner's Guide to Building Construction** introduces the principles of construction, providing the knowledge that is essential for making a success of any building job, whether a small home extension or a complete structure, from the foundation to the roof and drains.

Fuel and power costs are an increasing worry for every householder. **Beginner's Guide to Home Energy Saving** gives down-to-earth guidance on minimising the bills. Possibilities described range from no-cost 'energy housekeeping' measures to investments, large and small, in insulation and other improvements – not forgetting possible snags and side-effects. **Beginner's Guide to Central Heating** provides an understanding of central heating in its many forms, so that both intending owners and existing owners whose heating equipment needs replacing can choose the most effective and economical system. The author also gives advice on efficient heating control.

These are all available from bookshops. The series also includes guides to various craft and hobby subjects such as radio and electronics, photography and computers. New titles are added continually, and a colour brochure is available from:

NOTES